A STUDY IN THE DIALECTICS OF SPHOṬA

A STUDY
IN
THE DIALECTICS OF SPHOTA

GAURINATH SASTRI

MOTILAL BANARSIDASS
Delhi :: Varanasi :: Patna

Revised New Edition : Delhi, 1980

ISBN: 978-81-2082-778-3

Also available at:

MOTILAL BANARSIDASS
41 U.A. Bungalow Road, Jawahar Nagar, Delhi 110 007
8 Mahalaxmi Chamber, Warden Road, Mumbai 400 026
120 Royapettah High Road, Mylapore, Chennai 600 004
Sanas Plaza, Subhash Nagar, Pune 411 002
16 St. Mark's Road, Bangalore 560 001
8 Camac Street, Calcutta 700 017
Ashok Rajpath, Patna 800 004
Chowk, Varanasi 221 0011

PRINTED IN INDIA

BY JAINENDRA PRAKASH JAIN AT SHRI JAINENDRA PRESS,
A-45 NARAINA, PHASE I, NEW DELHI 110 028
AND PUBLISHED BY NARENDRA PRAKASH JAIN FOR
MOTILAL BANARSIDASS PUBLISHERS PRIVATE LIMITED,
BUNGALOW ROAD, DELHI 110 007

॥ श्रीः ॥

फणिपतिभणितीनां सारसर्वस्ववेदी
समजनि शिवसूनुः कोऽपि नागेशभट्टः ।
जगति यदुदिताभिः सन्निबन्धप्रभाभिः
सुरभयति दिगन्तान् वाङ्मयः कल्पवृक्षः ॥१॥

तदनुगुणगुणाढ्यः पायगुण्डेकुलाब्धेः
सितकर इव शिष्यस्तस्य विद्यैकतानः ।
समभवदुदितश्रीर्भूरिलेखानुबन्ध-
प्रमुदितबुधवृन्दो बालभट्टाभिधानः ॥२॥

तच्छिष्यक्रमतो मतो मतिमतां जातो मनीषावशा-
न्नव्यव्याकरणार्णवप्रमथने बद्धादरो मन्दरः ।
काशीनाथसुधीस्तदीयचरणध्यानावधानैकधी
राजारामबुधाग्रणीः शिवपुरे शिष्यो विशिष्यार्चितः ॥३॥

विश्वेश्वरः स्वयमुपात्ततनुस्तदीयं
शिष्यत्वमाप निखिलागमरक्षणाय ।
बाल्येऽपि यत्प्रतिभया वशितान्तरङ्गै-
र्नामाऽभ्यधीयत च बालसरस्वतीति ॥४॥

दिङ्मूलचुम्बितपदाम्बुरुहेषु तस्य
गङ्गाधरप्रभृतिशिष्यधुरन्धरेषु ।
प्राथम्यमाप विमलप्रतिभावतारो
मिश्रः क्षितौ शिवकुमारधरामरेन्द्रः ॥५॥

प्रतिवादिशैलहृदयं वाग्विशिखैर्विदलयन सहसा ।
विबुधचमूसेनानी रेजे श्रीशिवकुमारशास्त्रिवरः ॥६॥

तद्भक्तिपूतहृदयः सदयो जनेषु
हाराणचन्द्र इति विश्रुतनामधेयः ।
सांयात्रिकः सकलशास्त्रमहार्णवेषु
मान्यो गुरुर्जयति मे रचनावदान्यः ॥७॥

तत्सूक्तिनिर्झरनिमज्जनतः प्रसन्ने
चेतोमये स्फुरति यन्मुकुरे मदीये ।
सारस्वताध्वनि तदेव लिपिप्रबन्ध-
सत्कल्पनामयमुपायनमातनोमि ॥८॥

वाग्देवीकरुणापाङ्गसङ्गता विदुषां मुदे ।
कृतिरेषा चिरायास्तु श्रीगौरीनाथशास्त्रिणः ॥९॥

ISBN: 8120827783

CONTENTS

PREFACE

I

To discuss the nature of 'word' or more precisely, 'significant word' (*upādāna-śābda*) is a problem that has arrested the attention of Indian philosophers for centuries. Words are used to convey meanings. Now, a word in common parlance is not anything but the sum-total of a few letters and a sentence, which is usually held to be the unit of our thoughts and expressions, is an aggregate of a few words. On a careful and scientific analysis, however, it appears that a combination of letters forming a word and, likewise, a combination of words forming a sentence is never possible. Life of letters is only of short duration as they die out the next moment after they are pronounced. And, as a combination of objects is possible only in the case of their coexistence, it is not understood how an aggregate of a few letters making up a word or that of some words forming a sentence is obtainable. If it, however, be presumed that letters are not short-lived entities but are endowed with permanent existence, a combination of letters constituting a word may be conceivable but the manner in which such combination is to be achieved for purposes of expression of meaning remains to be studied in detail. The Naiyāyikas who believe in the evanescent character of letters and the Mīmāṁsakas who are advocates of their eternal character have in their own ways attempted to return suitable answers to the objections that at times seem to have been baffling. But, it is worthy of notice that the grammarians do not find them suitable for acceptance. They adumbrate a theory strikingly original to claim that both word and meaning are indivisible units. The indivisible unit of expression is called *sphoṭa* and the indivisible unit of meaning is also called *sphoṭa* or *pratibhā*. The grammarians do not believe that a word is divisible into letters or a sentence is divisible into words. Likewise, they do not believe that the meaning of a sentence is the sum-total of the meaning of words which are ordinarily described as its parts.

In order to understand and appreciate the merits of the theory postulated by the grammarians with great gusto and trenchant logic, one must acquaint oneself with the metaphysical background of their philosophy. It is said of Bhartṛhari, the most outstanding grammarian-philosopher second only in importance to Patañjali, the author of the *Vyākaraṇa-Mahābhāṣya* on the *Sūtras* of Pāṇini that in the course of his study of the problems of grammar, he happened to discuss the unfolding of the objective world from the Eternal Verbum (*Śabda-tattva, Śabda-Brahman, or Sphoṭa*). And, Bhaṭṭoji-Dīkṣita, in his *Śabda-kaustubha*, likens this event to the finding of a priceless gem in one's quest of an insignificant cowrie[1]. While we admire the poetic value of the analogy, we would yet prefer to go the other way around to opine that as Bhartṛhari was bred and brought up amidst monistic traditions, it was only possible for him to propound his favourite theory for purely empirical purposes as well. Bhartṛhari states that Veda is the means for the attainment of the Indescribable One or the Transcendent Reality,[2] which is beyond all limitations of time (*anādi-nidhanam*)[3] and space (*akṣaram*: derived from √*aś*, to pervade).[4] In the opening verse of the *Vākyapadīya* he introduces this Indescribable One as *brahman* and *śabda-tattva*. This, as we shall presently see, is in strict conformity with an important Vedic tradition according to which *brahman* and *vāk* are held to be conterminous.[5] The expression *brahman* (derived from √vṛh, to grow, to expand, to become great) means expanded consciousness of the individuated self. In the language of the Upaniṣads it is *pratyak-caitanya* (the individual soul) that becomes *brahma-caitanya* (the universal soul). This happens under the influence of divine afflatus. The Great God, says the Veda, comes to possess the mortal being.[6] This synchronises with the manifestation of *vāk* in the individual self. The first manifestation is in the form of a flash of spiritual illumination where expression and thought remain completely identified beyond any recognition. The second manifestation is in the form of an internal discourse (*antas-saṃjalpa*) where they remain welded together to constitute a homogeneous identity. The third and final stage is of articulate speech-forms where expression and meaning remain separate, the two being linked together as denoter (*vācaka*) and denotation (*vācya*).

According to Vedic traditions, as we have mentioned before, consciousness is word. With the expansion of consciousness *vāk* is externalized. In the process of externalization, however, *vāk* does not forfeit its own character; and, as such, it is looked upon as the image of the Indescribable One.[7] This being so, the Vedic lore owing its genesis to the intuitive light of expanded consciousness under divine afflatus is regarded as authoritative, infallible and unimpeachable. It is described that seers in their inspired mood have felt the urge of communicating their experience to those who are not as yet blessed with the vision of the Transcendent.[8] It may be remembered in this context that *vāk* does not reveal herself to all and sundry but chooses to bestow her favour on a few who are considered fit for the vision.[9]

We have stated that Bhartṛhari has elaborated the Vedic tradition when he describes the Absolute as *brahman* and *śabdatattva.* But, may we go a step further to point out that he introduces it as *akṣara* too. Usually, the expression *akṣara* means that which does not change or perish, i.e., unchanging or imperishable. The Transcendent is viewed as the prius of the universe that comes out of it but it remains constant in spite of those transformations. But, as it has been noticed before that the word may be derived from √*aś*, to pervade, meaning thereby 'what is pervasive and ubiquitous'. In this way the identity between *brahman* and *akṣara* may be understood. And, if *brahman* and *śabdatattva* are conterminous, it is understandable how the Indescribable One is described as *brahman, śabdatattva* and *akṣara.* The term *akṣara* is almost invariably used in Vedic literature as an adjective of *vyoman* or *parama-vyoman.*[10] The sky, to our knowledge, possesses maximum pervasion. It is why the Upaniṣads often describe *brahman* as the sky. In this context let us turn our attention to the oft-quoted line of the Kena-Upaniṣad where it is stated that Indra came across a female figure in that sky. This female figure is highly resplendent (*bahu-śobhamānām*) and adorned with gold ornaments (haimavatīm, which may mean 'daughter of the Himalayas' as well). She is described as Umā. Umā may be a proper name as Śaṅkara thinks. But, may we suggest that like *haimavatīm* and *bahuśobhamānām*, *umām* may be read as an adjective to *striyam* which seems to be the substantive here. The two words *umā* and *vyoman* bear affinity of meaning and are close to each other. The word *umā*, from √*av*, to protect, is used frequently as an adjective in RV. *Oman*, meaning 'favour' has been used more than once. The word *vyoman*, the sky, is derived from *vi-oman*, meaning 'unrestricted favour and protection'. A study of the aforesaid forms may enable us to posit that the two words *umā* and *vyoman* may be linked together, *umā* signifying one who grants favour and protects. And, if the locus or the female so described be the sky or *brahman* we may be warranted in drawing an identification between *umā*, the power of the sky and *vāk*, the power of *brahman*. It may be noted here that the realization of this power is possible only when she is pleased to extend the favour.

We have said that *akṣara* is used with reference to *parama-vyoman*; but, it may be mentioned that it is used with reference to *vāk* as well.[11] So, the conclusion is that *akṣara* denotes both *brahman* (parama-vyoman) and *vāk*. And, we all know that *brahman* and *vāk* form a divine couple. So, when Bhartṛhari asserts that the Indescribable is *brahman*, *śabdatattva* and *akṣara*, he restates and unfolds one of the most important concepts of the Vedic age.[12] And, we are all aware of his unflinching faith in the teachings of the Veda. He is eloquent on the value and importance of the Veda and its authority.

The first half *verse* of the opening verse of the *Vākyapadīya* sets forth what has been called the *svarūpa-lakṣaṇa* (what states the essential characteristics) of the Absolute in Monistic Vedānta while the other half-*verse* mentions the *taṭastha lakṣaṇa* (what states the accidental characteristics). The Absolute is the prius of the world. Though *brahman* has been likened to *ākāśa*, it is not absolute void. This *ākāśa* which the Absolute is, possesses a plurality of powers of which *kāla*, the power of independence, is the supreme.[13] Thus, the Absolute in the system of Bhartṛhari is a dynamic principle. It produces the universe out of itself. It appears to be the material and the efficient cause of all that exists. Although Śaṅkara would call the Absolute the material and efficient cause in one, the concept of causality is not applicable to it in absolute reality. If the metaphysical position of Śaṅkara was to be expressed in exact terminology, *brahman* would be said to appear as the cause and not to be the cause in absolute reality of the world. The position of the grammarians follows, of course, from the conception of the Absolute as endowed with the multiple powers which are as real as the Absolute.[14]

The attainment of the Absolute, the Great One, is described by Bhartṛhari in the following manner : the empirical self which is the logical and epistemological subject on this side of transcendental realization becomes united to the Ultimate Reality.[15] The Absolute, which is poetically described as the Great Bull, is there in all individuals, a self-identical principle, uniform, unchanging and steadfast spiritual light. The spiritual aspirant is led to the attainment of this light when he is freed from all bonds and limitations. Bhartṛhari calls this attainment as one of union, *sāyujya*. Obviously, this is the merging of the individual soul in the World-soul. The former becomes completely identified with the latter, the one with multiple powers. With the expansion of the individual consciousness brought about by some divine afflatus, all knots of egoism are torn asunder, all limitations of the individuated self fade away and the individual self finds himself completely expanded. I am *brahman*—this is how he declares.

The aforesaid conception of *sāyūjya* may be traced in the Veda.[16] Kātyāyana in his *anukramaṇikā* to RV. says that the Sun is the only Ṛgvedic God.[17] The Vedic seer yearns after attainment of union with the Sun. In one of the hymns of the *Vājasaneya Saṃhitā*, this yearning has found the most eloquent expression.[18] This idea has found maximum expression in the literature of the Upaniṣads where the identity of the individual soul with the World Soul has been established.[19]

II

Attempts have been made from time to time to hold that the sphoṭa-theory can claim a respectable antiquity. In one of the *Sūtras* of Pāṇini one comes across the name of an ancient grammarian, Sphoṭāyana,[20] who is presumed to be the pioneer in the field of the theory of *sphoṭa*. Whatever may be the merits of this hypothesis, one may still be quite sure that Patañjali knows *sphoṭa* as an eternal identity distinguishable from sound.[21] It was, however, for Bhartṛhari, the author of the *Vākyapadīya* and the *Prakīrṇa*, as also of a commentary on the *Mahābhāṣya*, to propound the theory of *sphoṭa* in a systematic manner. It was Kumārila-bhaṭṭa, the Mīmāṁsaka, and Jayanta-bhaṭṭa, the Naiyāyika, to offer searching criticism of the *sphoṭa*-theory and finally explain and uphold the cause of letters as constituents of significant words. The objections raised by Kumārila have, however, been squarely met by Maṇḍana Miśra in his *Sphoṭasiddhi.* He has, for obvious reasons, drawn his inspiration from what is recorded in Bhartṛhari's *Vākyapadīya.* It is necessary, therefore, to obtain, in particular, an acquaintance with the works of these four masters mentioned above in order to understand the nature of significant words and the manner in which meaning is expressed by them. In later years Koṇḍabhaṭṭa in his *Vaiyākaraṇa-bhūṣaṇa* and Nāgeśabhaṭṭa in his *Vaiyākaraṇa-siddhānta-laghu-mañjūṣā* have discussed *sphoṭa* and its classifications in some detail.

It is, however, very significant that Bhartṛhari's theory of *sphoṭa* has been studied and criticized by all the important writers in different branches of Indian Philosophy including Śabarasvāmin, Śaṅkarācārya and Vācaspati Miśra. We have, therefore, taken great care in presenting the *sphoṭa*-theory with as much precision as possible. The present work has been remodelled by us on the basis of an earlier work on the subject written and published more than four decades ago. (*The Journal of the Department of Letters*, Calcutta University, Vol. xxix).

It would be in the fitness of things to mention here that the author was deeply impressed and benefitted by the excelling pattern of dissertations on *Sphoṭa* and *Ṣabdabrahman* obtainable in the *Nyāyamañjarī* of Jayanta-bhaṭṭa in the beginning of his pursuits in the field. It is quite known to students of Indian philosophy that Jayanta-bhaṭṭa excels his rivals in the art of reviewing the position of his opponents with unimpeachable accuracy before he embarks upon advancing his own criticism. He does not seem to be satisfied unless he holds up in clear perspective the intentions of his adversary in a manner that looks prima facie invulnerable and it is then and then only that he revels in exposing the weaknesses which are often almost unanswerable. It has to be admitted that so long as Maṇḍana's *Sphoṭa-siddhi* was not published it was indeed very difficult to understand and appreciate the view of the grammarian-philosopher with requisite precision as both the text of the *Vākyapadīya* and the most cryptic commentary on it published from Vārāṇasī would hardly be intelligible and satisfying the needs of scholars anxious to delve deep into the intricate issues of the subject. To come back to the point, Jayanta-bhaṭṭa has given us the most searching analysis of the concept of *Sphoṭa*; he has unfolded with meticulous care and elucidated the advantages which it can claim before he starts his arguments in favour of the popular view that it is letters that are expressive of meaning. It must be acknowledged that while presenting the view of the grammarians' theory of *Sphoṭa* the present writer has supplemented his exposition wherever convenient and necessary by putting his thoughts assimilated from the text of the *Nyāyamañjarī*. But, it needs to be pointed out that he has taken upon himself the difficult task of meeting all the points discussed by the master to bring out the deeper implications of Bhartṛhari's theory for the first time and he has restated the almost unique position of the grammarians so that the academic world of to-day may appreciate how far a modern mind can associate itself with the currents of thought that have been flowing in this land of ours for centuries and give a new orientation that may be adjudged as a piece of original and substantial research by the coming generation of scholars in this country and abroad. It should be stated here that without the most inspiring guidance of Mahāmahopādhyāya Haran Chandra Sastri of hallowed memory it would not have been possible to engage oneself in this most arduous task and one is privileged to remember one's beloved *guru* at this hour of supreme satisfaction when the book is being presented to the academic world.

The author is pleased to remind the academic world in Indological Studies that his *Philosophy of Word and Meaning* published in the Calcutta Sanskrit College Series of Texts and Studies has so much inspired present-day writers that quite a substantial volume of literature on the subject has come into existence in our country and the West in the span of a little over a quarter of a century. Emboldened by the interest evinced by scholars working in the field, the present work, a revised one, is placed before them in the hope that it would provide them with an information about thoughts that have been inspiring our scholars for about some hundreds of years. In modern times, it is felt that the science of philology is being studied all over the academic world with a good deal of earnestness. But, it needs to be mentioned that ours is not a historical study; we have been modest enough to confine our attention to a presentation of the dialectics only and in our endeavour we have stated the different points of view as faithfully and critically as possible. We know our limitations; but, we are privileged to record that the complexities have nowhere been avoided; to the contrary, they have been sought to be ironed out to the best of human efforts.

III

The author is greatly indebted to Dr. Giorgio Rosso Cicogna and Dr. Carolina Rosso Cicogna, Licenciée en Langues Romanes, University of Louvain, for all the kind assistance and help that they have rendered in connection with the publication of this book, the former by arranging for his stay in the Capital during the period the book was in the press and the latter by assisting him in the reading of proofs. He is thankful to the publishers without whose active initiative the book would not have come out. Particular mention must be made of Sri M. Ramakrishna Sastry, M. A. M. Litt., for his voluntary assistance in this respect.

GAURINATH

DETAILED NOTICE OF CONTENTS

[Numbers in Antique refer to pages]

INTRODUCTION **1-16**

Two kinds of words — significant words (*upādāna-śabda*) — two elements of a significant word : the elements of sound and logos, the real word — sound reveals the real word while the genesis of sound is inspired by the latter—the real word or logos, also called *sphoṭa*, is the one that expresses meaning, **1**; word, a self-revealing entity—the grammarians' position is analogous to that in Monistic Vedānta — though *sphoṭa* is revealed by sound, still it does not forfeit its character of self-luminosity, **1**; the anomaly, if any, is resolved when it is said that even a self-revealing entity like Brahman requires the aid of cognitive instruments to remove the veil of nescience before it could reveal itself, **1-2**; relation between word and sound—sphoṭa is a unitary principle, it is sequenceless while sound is vicarious—properties of sound, those of sequence and plurality, are superimposed on *sphoṭa* — this is inevitable as the vision of *sphoṭa* without sound is never possible, **2**; Bhartṛhari illustrates how the character of plurality and sequence relating to sound is reflected *in sphoṭa*, **3**; three different views on how sound helps in the manifestation of *sphoṭa* — the first view : sounds produced by the vocal apparatus are cognized by the auditory organs — the second view : sounds at first reveal *sphoṭa* which is comprehended by the auditory organ later on — the third view : sound preparing the auditory organ to be receptive and serving to reveal *sphoṭa* seems to be Bhartṛhari's view, **3**; Kumārila mentions the above three views without acknowledging *sphoṭa* but maintains the eternality of word, **3**; Śabara's view—Śāntarakṣita's criticism, **4**; correspondence between the views of Kumārila and Bhartṛhari, illustrations, **4**; comprehension of *sphoṭa* does not require the cognition of sounds as a condition—metaphysical existence of *sphoṭa* not denied but not perceived on account of the distance separating it from the cognising subject, **5**; Bhartṛhari appears to be in favour of the first view—reasons offered, **5**; comprehension of *sphoṭa* explained—unitary identity of *sphoṭa* challenged, **6**; gradual manifestation of the same *sphoṭa* explained and the illustration of repeated recitation of a verse confirming the identity—weakness in the above explanation pointed out **5-6**; in case the same *sphoṭa* is gradually revealed, the justification for producing subsequent sounds beyond the first to be mentioned for, **6**; qualitative difference in each act of manifestation of *sphoṭa* held, **7**; the qualitative difference of the revelations as received by the mind involves no logical incongruity, **7**; the degrees of difference purely subjective, not warranting postulation of any difference in the objective nature of the essence of *sphoṭa*, **7**; letters and not *sphoṭa* are revealed : says the opponent — the grammarians' reply that *sphoṭa* is not revealed in its own nature when the individual sounds are produced but comes to be presented as such at the final stage not tenable, **8**; the opponent exposes the

ABBREVIATIONS

APB.	Āpastambaparibhāṣā (edited by S. Sāmaśramin)
AS.	Advaitasiddhi (Calcutta)
A. Sam.	Arthasaṁgraha (Chowkhamba Sanskrit Series Benares)
BB.	Bṛhadāraṇyakopaniṣat (Anandasrama Sanskrit Series, Poona 1902)
BP.	Bhāṣāpariccheda (Nirnayasagara Press, Poona 1916)
C. Read.	Logic, Deductive and Inductive
Din.	Dinakarī, commentary on SM. (Nirnayasagara Press, Poona, 1916)
Gop.	Gopālikā (Madras University Sanskrit Series, N. 6)
JNM.	Jaiminīyanyāyamālā (Anandasrama Sanskrit Series, Poona 1892)
Kāś.	Kāśikā (edited by B. Śāstrin, 2nd edition)
MB.	Mahābhāṣya of Patañjali (Nirnayasagara Press, Poona, 1917)
MBP.	Mahābhāṣyapradīpa (Nirnayasagara Press, 1917)
MK	Mādhyamikakārikā (Bibliotheca Buddhica)
MS.	Mīmāṁsāsūtras
Nir.	Nirukta (edited by S. Sāmaśramin)
NK.	Nyāyakandalī (Vizianagram Sanskrit Series)
N. Ku.	Nyāyakusumāñjali (Chowkhamba Sanskrit Series)
NM.	Nyāyamañjarī (Vizianagram Sanskrit Series)
NP.	Nyāyaprakāśa (edited by K. Nyāyapañcānana, Calcutta)
Pāṇ. Sū.	Pāṇinisūtras
PLM.	Paramalaghumañjūṣā (Chowkhamba Sanskrit Series)
PM.	Padamañjarī (edited by D. Śāstrin, 1898)
PNT.	Pramāṇanayatattvālokālaṅkāra
PSS.	Paribhāṣenduśekhara (Anandasrama Sanskrit Series)
RKT	Ratnākarāvatārikā, commentary on PNT.
RVB.	Ṛgvedabhāṣyopakramaṇikā (Sanskrit Sahitya Pariṣat Series, Calcutta)
Śab. K.	Śabdakaustubha (Asiatic Society of Bengal)
Sāṅ. Sū.	Sāṅkhyasūtras

Śār. Bh.	Śārīrakabhāṣya (Nirnayasagara Press, 1917)
ŚB.	Śabarabhāṣya (Anandasrama Sanskrit Series)
SC.	Sphoṭacandrikā of Kṛṣṇabhaṭṭa
SD.	Sāhityadarpaṇa (edited by R. Tarkavāgīśa, 1303 B.S., Calcutta)
Ś. Dīp.	Śāstradīpikā (Nirnayasagara Press)
SDS.	Sarvadarśanasaṁgraha (Anandasrama Sanskrit Series)
S. Kau.	Siddhāntakaumudī (Nirnayasagara Press, 1908)
SM.	Siddhāntamuktāvalī of Viśvanātha (Do., 1916)
SS.	Sphoṭasiddhi (Madras University Sanskrit Series, No. 6)
SS. (Bh.)	Sphotasiddhi of Bharatamiśra
SSN.	Sphoṭasiddhinyāyavicāra
ŚŚP.	Śabdaśaktiprakāśikā (Benares Tara Printing Works, 1907)
ŚV.	Ślokavārttika (Chowkhamba Sanskrit Series)
TB.	Tattvabindu (Do., 2nd edition)
T. Bod.	Tattvabodhinī, commentary on S. Kau. (Nirnayasagara Press, 1908)
TS.	Tattvasaṁgraha
VBS.	Vaiyākaraṇabhūṣaṇasāra (Chowkhamba Sanskrit Series)
VBSD.	Vaiyākaraṇabhūṣaṇasāradarpaṇa, commentary on VBS. (Chowkhamba Sanskrit Series)
VKP.	Vedāntakalpataruparimala, super-commentary on Śār. Bh. (Nirnayasagara Press, 1917)
VP.	Vākyapadīya (Benares Sanskrit Series)
VPS.	Vākyapadīya, (Poona 1966)
VPar.	Vedāntaparibhāṣā (Calcutta University publication)
VSLM.	Vaiyākaraṇasiddhāntalaghumañjūṣā (edited by G. Śarman)
YS.	Yogasūtras
YSV.	Vyāsabhāṣya on Yogasūtras (Bombay Sanskrit and Prakrit Series)

INTRODUCTION

TWO KINDS OF WORDS

The opening chapter of the *Vākyapadīya*, known as *Brahma-kāṇḍa* (or *Āgama-samuccaya*) discusses the nature of 'word' (*śabda, sphoṭa, logos*) and its relation to 'sound' (*dhvani, nāda*). The grammarian recognises two kinds of significant words (*upādāna-śabda*); of the two, one is said to be the cause of sound while the other is associated with the meaning.[1] According to the grammarian, there are two elements in each significant word, the element of sound and the element of logos, the real word, which possesses meaning and significance of its own. Sound reveals the real word while its genesis is inspired by the latter. The logos or the real word is ever present in the mind and as such it cannot be apprehended by another mind unless it is conveyed by appropriate sounds. Sounds are primarily concerned with the task of revealing the real word and once this is done, the meaning is automatically expressed. Owing to our uncritical habits of understanding we fail to distinguish between the two with the result that we believe that it is sound that expresses meaning.[2]

WORD : A SELF-REVEALING IDENTITY

The grammarian describes 'word' the ever-present principle, as a self-luminous identity. To all intents and appearances, his position is analogous to that of the Monistic Vedāntist. The grammarian likens *sphoṭa* to the light that reveals itself as well as the object that comes into contact with it.[3] *Sphoṭa*, likewise reveals itself and at the time of self-revelation it reveals sounds as well. So, when it is said that *sphoṭa* is revealed by sound what is meant is that sounds that owe their genesis to *sphoṭa* reveal it to other minds. Understood in this sense *sphoṭa* or *logos* does not forfeit its character of self-luminosity even though it is held that the same is revealed by sounds.

Let us pursue the point in detail. The apparent anomaly is dissolved if the analogy between the two systems of Monistic Vedānta and Grammar on the Absolute is rigorously pursued.

We, finite beings, with our various limitations cannot have a vision of the Ultimate Reality, the *Brahman*, a self-revealing principle without the help of cognitive instruments (*pramāṇa*) that alone can remove the veil of nescience that shrouds it. Likewise, *sphoṭa*, though self-revealing in nature, baffles our cognition unless sounds reveal it. It is because of our inborn ignorance that it is never possible to cognise a self-revealing entity like *sphoṭa* without any extraneous assistance, the assistance that is rendered by sounds. So, the position that *sphoṭa* is revealed by sounds is not in the least incompatible with the one that *sphoṭa* is a self-luminous identity, that it reveals its own self as well as sounds.

From what has been said above, it appears that the grammarian approaches the subject not only from the transcendental but also from the empirical point of view, taking in account both the metaphysical nature of the Ultimate Reality, the Word-Spirit (*Śabda-tattva*) and the pattern of its realization in our everyday life with the gradual emergence of correct knowledge and the corresponding disappearance of ignorance to which every human being is more or less subject. It remains to be said that the limitations of the cognising subject are responsible for the transference of the properties or attributes of sounds to *sphoṭa* to which they do not actually belong.

RELATION BETWEEN WORD AND SOUND

According to Bhartṛhari, *sphoṭa* is a unitary principle that transcends division. As such, it is held to be a sequenceless (*akrama*) identity. Sound, on the other hand, is vicarious as it is produced at different times through different efforts. The notions of sequence and plurality are wrongly attributed to *sphoṭa*. The relation between sounds and *sphoṭa* has been declared to be one of the manifestor and the manifested and it is the attributes of the manifestor, its plurality and sequence, that are mirrored in the manifested, which, notwithstanding its unitary and sequenceless character, seems to be endowed with plurality and sequence. The character of sounds overshadows the real identity of *sphoṭa*. To be explicit, it is sounds that are either short or long, palatal, cerebral or nasal. But, *sphoṭa* remains unaffected all the time. The confusion arises because we cannot obtain the vision of *sphoṭa* without sounds.[4]

Bhartṛhari explains this fact with apt illustrations. Thus, he says that the moon shining above in the blue canopy of the sky is one and fixed, but when she is reflected in the dancing ripples of the lake down below, do we not see a thousand and one moons all moving about in the water?[5] What is one appears to be many, what is fixed appears to be unsteady and full of movement. It is practically impossible on our part to imagine that the moon shining above is one and fixed when our eyes are riveted on the ripples that have caught the reflection. Likewise, *sphoṭa* or *śabda-tattva* is one and eternal and the character of plurality or of sequence is but superimposed on it. So long as *sphoṭa* lies embedded in the intellect, it is like the fluid in the peacock's egg (*mayūrāṇḍa-rasavat*) with all its potentialities lying hidden.[6] At that stage, *sphoṭa* is one and divisionless — it is a homogeneous entity. But, as soon as one feels the urge of conveying one's thoughts to others, *sphoṭa* finds expression through sounds in the shape of letters, words and sentences, and as this is the practice current from time immemorial, one confuses the real characters of *sphoṭa* and sounds. And, in the absence of a proper and correct understanding of the real situation, one invariably fails to distinguish between the two and their individual characteristics.

It has been said in a preceding paragraph that sounds help *sphoṭa* in its self-manifestation and the grammarian tells us how this help is rendered. Bhartṛhari records three different views on this point including one of his own. According to the first view, sounds are produced by the vocal apparatus and when they are cognised by the auditory organ, they become instrumental in manifesting *sphoṭa*. The second view states that sounds at first reveal *sphoṭa* which is subsequently comprehended by the auditory organ. There is yet another view according to which sounds prepare the auditory organ to be receptive and serve to reveal *sphoṭa* as well.[7] Bhartṛhari seems to be an upholder of this last view.

It may be quite interesting to remember that though the Mīmāṁsist does not acknowledge *sphoṭa* and still believes in the eternality of words and their manifestation through sounds, yet he maintains that the manifestation of words is possible in three ways. Thus, Kumārila says that the manifestation is possible through a change (*saṁskāra*) in the word itself, or through a change in the sense-organ (the ear), or through both.[8] Śabara svāmin has, of course, mentioned the first alternative only and he has been strongly criticised by Śāntarakṣita, the celebrated Buddhist scholar, in his *Tattva-saṁgraha*. If we closely study the views of Bhartṛhari and Kumārila referred to above, we shall find that they agree in saying that the manifestation of word is possible in three ways; they differ only in this that word to Bhartṛhari means *sphoṭa*, while to Kumārila it is the combination of letters. Now, let us examine why the two great masters opine that the manifestation may be in three ways only, neither more nor less. The point is that a particular action sometimes acts upon or benefits the sense-organ (*indriya*), while at other times, it is the object (*viṣaya*) and not the sense-organ that happens to enjoy the fruit of an action and occasions are not rare when the action helps both the sense-organ and the object.

The point may be explained with the help of appropriate illustrations. Concentration of the mind or application of collyrium enables or strengthens our eyes to see objects. In either case, therefore, it is the cognitive instrument that enjoys the benefit. But, when the ground is watered and we perceive some smell, it is not that the watering of the ground has benefited the sense-organ (viz., the nostril) in any way. The water has evidently contributed some attribute to the ground whereupon the smell, heretofore unperceived, is now perceived. This is, therefore, a case in which the object and not the sense-organ is benefited. But, when we light a candle, the eye becomes competent to perceive an object lying hidden in the darkness and the object, too, becomes fit for being comprehended by the eye.[9] In this case, it is not possible for us to deny that the object has been benefited. For, it is a matter of common knowledge that a person standing in the open air where there is ample light, cannot see an object lying in the darkness. Here is an instance of both the sense-organ and the object having received benefit from the light. Bhartṛhari, likewise, maintains that sounds not only make the auditory organ receptive but reveal *sphoṭa* at the same time.

COMPREHENSION OF SPHOṬA AND SOUND

Having discussed the nature of the relation that subsists between *sphoṭa* and sound, Bhartṛhari proceeds to take up the problem — How are the two comprehended ? He states four different views on this point. Thus, he says, that according to some, *sphoṭa* is cognised as identical with sounds; the two cannot be comprehended separately with their individual distinctions completely kept apart and not intermingled.[10] Bhartṛhari's representation of this view has found a happy elucidation from the pen of the commentator who says that just as a piece of crystal appearing crimson in contact with a crimson *japā* flower (*hibiscus rosasinensis*), cannot be conceived without the colour contracted from the flower, so *sphoṭa* cannot be comprehended without the characteristics of sounds that invariably find their reflection in the former. According to the second view, the comprehension of *sphoṭa* does not require the cognition of sounds as a condition. The advocates of this theory seek to explain their position by saying that it is an established fact that the attributes or properties of the sense-organ are not required to be known for purposes of the cognition of the object (*viṣaya*). As we know, Patañjali describes sound as the attribute of *sphoṭa*, and it is contended, therefore, that sounds are not required to be known prior to the cognition of *sphoṭa* though the former is said to be indicative of the latter. There are again a few thinkers who believe in the metaphysical existence of *sphoṭa* but are of the opinion that, though existent, it is not perceived on account of the distance separating it from the cognising subject. We know that distance prevents perception of remote stars. Others do not deny the perceivability of *sphoṭa*, but think that distance does not remove it entirely from the ken of perception. It fails to be perceived as a distinct entity.[11]

Of the four views recorded above, the third and the fourth cannot find favour with Bhartṛhari for obvious reasons. For, he has specific discussion on the nature of the comprehension of *sphoṭa*, namely, whether it is distinct or otherwise. In his opinion, *sphoṭa* is comprehended and completely too. As for the second view that sounds cannot be cognised, it may be said that Bhartṛhari cannot have any sympathy for it. For, he has himself raised the problem whether there is any justification for admitting sound as well when *sphoṭa* is maintained to be the denoter (*vācaka*); and, in his answer to this problem, he states in clear terms that the existence of sounds, cannot be disowned in view of the fact that they are directly perceived. It is for this reason that we are inclined to think that the first view may be Bhartṛhari's own and the explanation put forward is in perfect accord with his doctrine.[12]

COMPREHENSION OF SPHOṬA EXPLAINED

We have discussed the nature of the two concepts, sound and *sphoṭa* and their relationship as well. It is now proposed to consider the problems of manifestation of *sphoṭa* more critically for a precise assessment of the position of the grammarian. The grammarian conceives *sphoṭa* as an indivisible unit. But, it is argued by the opponent that the unity of *sphoṭa* can hardly be upheld in the event of the supposition that it is revealed by sounds. To be explicit, it is pointed out that separate efforts are required to produce different sounds which in their turn are supposed to reveal *sphoṭa* and in view of the fact that sounds are produced in succession and not simultaneously, the comprehension of *sphoṭa* as a unitary identity requires to be explained.

In his attempt to answer the point the grammarian throws a flood of light on the deeper implications of his theory. To understand his point of view it will be convenient to take an illustration. It is maintained by Bhartṛhari that in the case of the word 'cow' each of the three sounds, viz., *c*, *o* and *w* reveals one and the same *sphoṭa* and it should not be misunderstood that the *sphoṭa*, which finds its expression through the medium of the three sounds mentioned above, is different on each occasion as the media of manifestation are different in nature. The grammarian is emphatic on this point that the same *sphoṭa* is manifested by each one of the three successive sounds differing from one another. The grammarian seeks to elucidate the point with the help of apt illustrations. Thus, he says that each time a Vedic chapter (*anuvāka*) or a particular verse is recited, the subsequent recitals do not create an impression that each time a new chapter or a new verse is recited which was not recited before; to the contrary, with each reading the identity becomes confirmed and distinction or difference, if any, vanishes. Likewise, in the present case, each one of the three sounds serves to manifest one and the same *sphoṭa* and there is hardly any room for an apprehension that the unity of *sphoṭa* cannot be understood.[13]

But, it needs to be pointed out that the explanation offered by the grammarian does not silence the opponent and the latter takes up the challenge to point out the weakness to which the explanation is exposed. The opponent raises this issue that when each one of the several sounds manifests one identical *sphoṭa*, there can be little justification for any effort or efforts to produce subsequent sounds. *Sphoṭa* is described as a partless identity and it is obvious that the whole *sphoṭa* is revealed by the initial sound. To utter other sounds for an identical purpose is totally unnecessary.

Bhartṛhari unfolds the niceties of his favourite theory in his attempt to answer the objection raised by the opponent. He admits without any reservation that each sound is competent to reveal the whole *sphoṭa*; but, he points out that there is a qualitative difference in each act of manifestation, the first one being somewhat indistinct while the remaining ones are more and more distinct. Thus, he enunciates that the preceding sounds leave their impressions on the mind and that it is the final sound reinforced by the previous impressions which acquires the maximum aptitude for a complete revelation of *sphoṭa*.

The primal revelation is indistinct and each succeeding revelation serves to make its apprehension more and more distinct. This additional efficacy of succeeding sounds is due to the impression left by each of the previous sounds on the mind which acquires progressively greater and greater aptitude for receiving further glimpses. The process comes to an end when the final sound is pronounced. It enables the mind which has acquired the adequate sensitiveness imparted by the previous impressions left by antecedent sounds to comprehend *sphoṭa* in its undimmed glory. It must be pointed out that *sphoṭa* does not possess any qualitative or quantitative difference. The qualitative difference of the revelations as received by the mind does not involve any logical incongruity. *Sphoṭa* is complete and perfect and does not admit of qualitative or quantitative addition or diminution. It is, no doubt, presented to the mind even by the first sound. But, the mind is so constituted that it must be trained to receive the full glimpse of *sphoṭa*. It should, therefore, be borne in mind that the degrees of difference are purely subjective due to the inherent constitution of the human intellect and they do not warrant us in postulating any such difference in the objective nature and essence of *sphoṭa*.[14]

CRITICISM BY THE OPPONENT

We have presented the view-point of the grammarian but it needs to be mentioned that the opponent does not as yet give ground and raise further difficulties to thwart the position that Bhartṛhari has taken up. Thus, he says that what is manifested by each of the sounds is but a letter and nothing else. For instance, in the case of the word "cow," the first sound does not reveal in an indistinct way the required *sphoṭa* in question nor the succeeding sounds reveal the same in a progressively distinct manner. The point is that the three sounds reveal the three letters, '*c*', '*o*' and '*w*' respectively. The grammarian may argue that *sphoṭa* is not revealed in its own nature when individual sounds are pronounced; it is then revealed in the shape of letters and it is only in the final stage that it comes to be presented as *sphoṭa*. But, it is argued that such a supposition is unnecessary on the ground that the initial appearance of *sphoṭa* as letters and the invariable subsequent manifestation of its reality as *sphoṭa* are mere postulations lacking adequate proof to justify them. Thus, it is laid down that wherever something *appears* to be different from what it *really* is, we must state the reason to account for the abnormality. In the present case, however, we cannot satisfactorily explain why a particular *sphoṭa* will not be at first manifested as such but as something different from it. We cannot maintain that sounds will be responsible for this unexpected appearance for the simple reason that they have been described to be giving us the knowledge of the *reality*, viz., *sphoṭa*. It is hardly justified to say that what gives us the knowledge of the *reality* is also competent to enable us to obtain the knowledge of the *appearance*; for the same cause can never give rise to two different effects under the same circumstances.

Moreover, it is a well-known fact that in all cases of the knowledge of the *appearance*, there cannot be any law restricting the *appearance* to showing itself invariably in the same form. Thus, it is a matter of common knowledge that the rope or the mother-o'-pearl does not of necessity appear as a snake or a piece of silver respectively. It is not uncommon that the rope is mistaken for a line of water or the mother-o'-pearl for something other than the white metal. Further, we cannot even maintain that a particular object should at all times invariably appear as something else. It is obvious that the rope is not always mistaken for a snake or the mother-o'-pearl for a piece of silver by all men alike.

BHARTṚHARI'S REPLY

Bhartṛhari, however, anticipated all these objections advanced by his opponents, and he sets forth his arguments to counteract them. Thus, he says that it is a fact that objects do at times appear as something quite different in nature from themselves. It is a piece of common knowledge that a tree observed from a distance appears to be an elephant and when a man enters a dark room from outside where there is much light, he mistakes the rope for a snake. But, on more close and careful observations at subsequent moments of time, the tree is recognised as such and the rope ceases to look like a snake any longer.[15] So, we must remember that careful observations on several occasions enable us to cognise a thing accurately and in its proper form; and that being so, we can scarcely afford to dispense with these observations as totally unnecessary and futile. On this analogy, Bhartṛhari says that *sphoṭa* appears as something different from itself when the first sound and the following ones excepting the final are pronounced; it is only when the final sound is uttered that *sphoṭa* appears in its real form.[16] It may be argued here that in cases of error, there is similarity between the *reality* and its *appearance*; but in the present case we cannot explain why *sphoṭa* is not revealed in its own nature when the first sound is pronounced. Maṇḍana in his *Sphoṭasiddhi* and following him, Vācaspati in his commentary on the *Vyāsabhāṣya* of the *Yogasūtras* of Patañjali, have stated that the effort required to produce a sound that manifests an isolated letter on the one hand and the one that serves to reveal a *sphoṭa* on the other, are somewhat similar in nature and it is because of this similarity that the latter appears as the former.[17] It is said that the effort required to produce a sound revealing the letter '*h*' is different from the effort necessary for uttering the sound which reveals the *sphoṭa* in "*han-*" or "*hananam*"; for the '*h*' in "*han*" or "*hananam*" is not a mere isolated unit having a reality by and in *itself* but finds its realisation within the *whole*. That being so, it becomes clear why an effort necessary to produce a sound that reveals an isolated letter is different from an effort needed to produce a sound that manifests a *sphoṭa*. But, as there is similarity between the two efforts, it becomes explicable why the latter appears as the former in spite of their differences.

The grammarian further points out that it is sounds and sounds only that serve to show *sphoṭa* as letters in the first instance and subsequently in its real nature. And, as he does not postulate any other phenomenon to account for the *appearance*, it is intelligible why the *appearance* invariably happens in the same way.

BHARTṚHARI UNFOLDS THE DEEPER IMPLICATIONS OF HIS THEORY

Bhartṛhari studies the aforesaid problem more intensely and throws further light on the inner significance of the position that he takes up. It is admitted on all hands that the knowledge of a number, say, 'three', depends upon the knowledge of its preceding number, viz., 'two.' But, the knowledge of the number 'three' is certainly different from that of 'two', and hence, when the knowledge of 'three' is obtained, we cannot say that the knowledge of 'two' is also present. Now, when the knowledge of 'two' is necessarily indispensable for the knowledge of 'three', we are constrained to admit that the knowledge of 'two' appears to be present, though it is not actually so and gives us the knowledge of 'three'. And, it is a matter of common knowledge that even *appearance* is capable of giving rise to *real* consequences. A man may die of heart-failure from the false knowledge that the rope is a snake. Coming to the point, we may observe that *sphoṭa* is manifested by the first sound but we fail to understand it on account of the limitations to which our intellect is subject. It happens that with the perception of the first sound, *sphoṭa* appears to be nothing other than a letter;[18] but, the knowledge of letter which is an *appearance* after all, serves as the medium giving us ultimately the knowledge of *sphoṭa*.

Bhartṛhari further strengthens his position by pointing out that whatever happens must pass through definite stages in course of its development or manifestation. Thus, the seed goes through several stages before it turns into a tree. The milk, too, before it changes into curd, gradually changes its form till the transformation is complete. Similarly, sounds reveal *sphoṭa* and before the latter is fully manifested, we must seek to realise it step by step.[19] But, Bhartṛhari does not stop here. In fact, the whole truth remains unsaid if he does not explain his point more fully. So, Bhartṛhari states, with all the boldness and perspicuity that he can command, that the process in which *sphoṭa* has been said to be revealed is postulated only to explain how the ordinary individual understands *sphoṭa*. But, it is a fact that the sages to whom the Eternal Light of *Śabda-brahman* has manifested itself, always understand *sphoṭa* without going through the course described above. To them the first sound manifests *sphoṭa* fully and completely. The *reality* dawns at the very outset and the question of *appearance* cannot arise under the circumstances. To understand *sphoṭa* with the perception of the first sound depends entirely upon the understanding power of the cogniser. Those who cannot understand it with the perception of the first sound must try to realise the same by some means or other; and, whatever these means are, they have their own value in so far as they enable us to have a vision of the *reality*.[20]

BHARTṚHARI ON PATAÑJALI'S CONCEPTION OF SPHOṬA

Bhartṛhari advances his criticism of the views of some thinkers who interpret Patañjali's conception of *sphoṭa* in a different way from what he himself has said. Patañjali has spoken 'of the' eternally established relation between 'word' (*śabda*) and import (*artha*).[21] And, when he says in that connection that 'word' is eternal, he means that word-ness, i.e., the universal inhering in all words, (*śabdatva*) is eternal. Now, word-ness pertains to all words and is, therefore, regarded as a class (*jāti*) and, so, it is said to be eternal. Now, if word-ness be regarded as a class, it has to be admitted that word-individuals (*śabda-vyakti*) are suggestive of word-ness. For, it is the individual (*vyakti*) that serves to manifest the class (*jāti*). According to this view, therefore, the word-individual should be conceived as being on a par with sounds which, according to Bhartṛhari, manifest *sphoṭa*.[22] Bhartṛhari, however, refuses to accept this view. To him, 'word' is not eternal because it is a class (*jāti*); but, it is so as an indivisible unity.

SPHOṬA : IS IT AN ETERNAL ENTITY ?

Bhartṛhari studies the views of some philosophers who opine that *sphoṭa* cannot be conceived of as an eternal entity. It is well known to a student of Indian Philosophy that there is a twofold conception of 'word', some holding that it is revealed while others maintaining that it is produced. It is contended that in either case, 'word' must be transient; for, whatever is revealed or produced is of an evanescent character. The jar is revealed to our view by the light and we know that the jar is subject to destruction. And, it goes without saying that an object which is produced must die one day. Bhartṛhari does not think it necessary to discuss the question of the production of 'word' but he makes a cogent answer to the statement that whatever is revealed must be non-eternal. Thus, he points out that it is an admitted fact that the class is manifested by the individual, but it is never asserted on that ground that the former is a non-eternal entity.[23]

MANIFESTATION OF SPHOṬA : IS IT TENABLE ?

It has been argued that the revelation of *sphoṭa* as explained by Bhartṛhari is not justified. For, it is an established fact that the manifestor and the manifested always reside in the same locus (*adhikaraṇa*). The light that reveals the jar must necessarily be present on the same spot where the jar is. We have never seen that the jar lying in our chamber is revealed to our view when a lamp is lit in another room separated from it by means of brick-walls or wooden partitions through which the light can hardly pass. If it is maintained that the relation between sounds and *sphoṭa* is one of the manifestor and the manifested, it follows that they reside in the same substratum. But, we know that *sphoṭa* lies in the mind while sounds are produced in the cavity of the mouth. And, as they, therefore, do not reside in the same place, we are hardly justified in saying that the aforesaid relation subsists between them.

Bhartṛhari steers clear of the difficulty when he points out that the analogy does not hold good; for, it is only in the case of concrete substances (*mūrta*) that the imposed condition is necessary. But, as neither *sphoṭa* nor sound has any concrete existence, the said condition cannot be legitimately demanded.[24]

TWO CLASSES OF SOUND

Having carefully explained the nature of *sphoṭa* and its relation to sounds, Bhartṛhari draws a line of demarcation between two classes of sounds. And, he says that sounds are of two types: one, *prākṛta* (the original sound) and the other, *vaikṛta* (the derivative transformation). The former is one without which the unmanifested *sphoṭa* cannot be comprehended while the latter enables the manifested *sphoṭa* to be comprehended for longer and longer moments of time without any cessation.[25] Though *nāda* and *dhvani* are generally regarded as one and the same thing, Bhartṛhari distinguishes between the two, and he says that the notion of sequence attributed to *sphoṭa* is after all due to *nāda* while it is the *prākṛta* sound that determines the question of its shortness or length. And, it should be remembered that the question of rapidity or prolongation is to be decided with reference to the *vaikṛta* sound.[26] The procedure seems to be an elaboration of the main thesis that sounds are only indicative of the metaphysical *sphoṭa* and the differences of sound do not have any bearing on the nature of *sphoṭa*. When we say that a word is short or long, we only ascribe the attribute, viz., shortness or length, attributes pertaining to *prākṛta* sounds, to *sphoṭa* which is one and indivisible. The nature of *vaikṛta* sounds has been explained by the commentator in the following way. When we beat a drum, the sound produced is heard from a long distance; but, when we strike a gong, the sound reaches only a short distance but it is heard for a longertime without cessation. The difference in the nature of these two sounds explains the conception of *vaikṛta* sound.[27] *Prākṛta* sounds, on the other hand, are what serve to manifest *sphoṭa* and are confounded with *sphoṭa* by the average man and philosophers of opposite schools.

DIFFERENT CONCEPTIONS OF WORD

Bhartṛhari concludes his observations on *sphoṭa* by referring to three well-known theories about the nature of word. It has been said by some that the internal air striking against the different vocal organs assume the state of word; while there are others who believe that word is made up of physical atoms. But, Bhartṛhari, following in the wake of Patañjali, observes that word is nothing but internal consciousness.[28] Patañjali in his *Mahābhāṣya* (on Pāṇ. Sū. I. iv. 29) suggests that the internal consciousness remains in the form of subtle speech and when it becomes manifest, it takes the form of word.

The first theory stated above is a very old one and we find that the ancient phoneticians speak of the internal air as the creative factor of word.[29] Śabara has rejected the theory on the ground that if words were air-products, we should have felt the air-atoms by touch.[30] The Naiyāyikas, too, have controverted the theory by pointing out that if words were air-products, they could be cognised only through the tactile organ. The auditory organ cannot be supposed to be made of air-atoms and, as such, it would be perfectly incompetent to envisage words. Moreover, if words or sounds be supposed to be made up of air-elements, they would be non-eternal. If words be conceived as the products of an aggregate of air-atoms or if they are thought to be attributes of air-atoms, they would be imperceptible like the tactile properties inhering in the same atoms. But, none of these alternatives can be entertained as a plausible theory simply because air-products are invariably perceived through tactile sensations and, certainly, it would be absolutely futile to make out that words or sounds are possessed of tactile properties, a supposition for which there is no warrant in experience.[31]

The grammarian, however, does not believe that word is made up of air particles inasmuch as word is an eternal entity.[32] It is sound or *dhvani* which is believed to be modifications of an airy substance. The objection of the Naiyāyika that airy particles cannot be perceived without their tactile qualities, does not seem to be cogent, as there is no restriction that all the qualities of a particular substance should be cognised together. Only, those properties which are evolved, are amenable to perception; otherwise, the non-perception of colour in hot air could not be explained. The next objection of the Naiyāyika is that sounds cannot be cognised through the auditory organ if they are believed to be airy (*vāyavīya*) in nature, because sense-organs are competent to perceive those qualities alone which belong to substances kindred to that of which sense-organs also are constituted. Thus, the eye perceives colour because colour is an attribute of fire which is also the formative principle of the visual organ. So, if sound be believed to be a property of air, it would be incapable of being perceived by the auditory organ as the latter is not made up of air. This objection has not been anticipated by the grammarian; and, so, we do not know the precise answer he might return to it.

The objection, however, can be refuted if we think that sounds are properties of ether and that length and pitch, intensity and feebleness, are the properties of sound and not of *sphoṭa* which is revealed by them. The objection of Udayana that these properties are invariably felt to be associated with words, and that the distinctive existence of words apart from sounds is not perceived, and that, therefore, is no proof for *sphoṭa*, has been fully discussed and refuted. The alleged non-perception cannot be regarded as a cogent argument against the possibility of *sphoṭa* which has been proved by abundant logic, and the empirical evidence is after all inconclusive.

Let us now discuss the theory of the atomic constitution of words referred to by Bhartṛhari. Though the commentators have not thrown any light on this theory, we are fortunately able to trace it to the Jaina system of thought. The Jainas believe that words are material substances made up of atoms which are distinct from other material atoms in nature. These atoms have been designated as sound-atoms in order to distinguish them from the acknowledged kinds of atoms, viz., air, earth, etc. The Naiyāyikas have criticised this theory on various grounds. The first objection is that words made up of an aggregate of atoms are not conceivable apart from tactile qualities. But, words are never cognised to be possessed of tactile properties. The second objection is that if words were possessed of mass, they could not but be obstructed by a barrier. Thirdly, there is no experience of the parts of a word. Fourthly, being possessed of corporeal magnitude, it should be felt to come into clash with other small particles and should, therefore, displace them. But, none of these possibilities is seen to be the case.

The Jainas, however, do not think these objections to be serious obstacles to their conception. Words may be conceived to be possessed of tactile qualities though these qualities may, by their very nature, remain unmanifested and, as such, may escape detection. This is quite evident from the fact that the perception of words is contingent upon the course of the wind and, so, with a forward wind distant words are perceived and when the course of the wind is in a different direction, even proximate words are intercepted from coming within the range of the auditory organ. It is easily explicable if words or sounds be supposed to be possessed of tactile properties like other material substances. The second objection, too, is unsubstantial. Because the influx and efflux of odorous particles are seen to take place even in a closed area though these odorous molecules are acknowledged to be possessed of magnitude. If, to escape this difficulty, it is assumed that these small particles are not prevented from effecting an entry through small apertures in the barriers, the same explanation can be offered by the Jainas. The third objection is also based upon a false analogy. Because, in such phenomena as a flash of lightning and the like, parts are not distinctly felt. So, the mere existence of parts is no guarantee for the perception of the same. Nor, again, non-perception of parts can be construed into evidence of their absence. The fourth objection, too, does not seem to be convincing as the alleged consequence is not seen to take place when odorous particles effect their entrance into the nasal membrane. These particles, in spite of their magnitude, do not shake the hairs in the nostrils. If extreme lightness is trotted out as an explanation in the case of odorous particles, the same may be accepted by the Jainas in the case of sound-molecules.

The grammarian, however, refuses to accept the Jaina theory exactly on the same grounds on which the Nyāya-Vaiśeṣika theory has been rejected. The postulation of an infinite number of sound-entities is in direct opposition to the recognition of identity of words. And, it has been sufficiently proved by the philosophical investigations that word is not anything distinct from consciousness and, as such, it is spiritual in nature. All the previous theories proceed upon a misconception of the fundamental nature and function of word.[33]

CHAPTER ONE

1. *Critique of the Objections from the Nyāya and Mīmāṁsā Schools*

NATURE OF WORD AND SENTENCE

Jayanta-bhaṭṭa opens the chapter on the authority of word (*śabda*) as a cognitive instrument (*pramāṇa*) by starting an enquiry into the nature of word and sentence. It is an established fact that sequence plays an important role in determining causal relation. And, Jayanta argues that it is a matter of common knowledge that the cognition of a word or a sentence is immediately succeeded by the cognition of its import. But, the difficulty, with which we are confronted, lies in determining the nature of the two terms 'word' and 'sentence.' It is generally maintained that a word comprises several letters while a sentence is nothing more than an aggregate of a few such words. But, on a critical examination of the real position it will appear that the definitions cited above are not strictly accurate.

VĀCASPATI'S PRESENTATION OF THE GRAMMARIAN'S THEORY

Vācaspatī-miśra in his *Tattva-bindu* observes that none can deny the fact that when several words constituting a sentence are cognised, we understand its import. But, the point arises : is the sense expressed by words themselves which are like so many individual units or is it expressed by the letters constituting those words ?

The Mīmāṁsakas believe in the eternal and all-pervading character of letters. And, Vācaspati rightly points out that it is for this reason that the Mīmāṁsakas cannot maintain that words admit of division into letters. The precise purport of Vācaspati's viewpoint may be expressed in the following way. It is a general rule that the magnitude of the whole (*avayavin*) is greater than that of its parts (*avayava*). But, if the all-pervading nature of letters is assumed and if letters be held to be the constituents of words, the magnitude of a word would be greater than that of the letters constituting it.[1] But, as the latter magnitude is assumed to be ubiquitous, the position would become absurd; for the composite word made up of such ubiquitous letters would come to occupy a magnitude which will be larger than that of its parts (i.e., letters). But, even if it be argued that such a magnitude being inconceivable, the whole in this case will not be possessed of a greater magnitude, as both the whole and its parts possess the maximum magnitude *ne plus ultra*, this, too, will lead to a preposterous issue; for the relation of the whole and its parts between two ubiquitous substances is logically absurd.[2]

Next, Vācaspati examines the position of the Vaiśeṣikas and says that if it, however, be assumed after them that sound and, for the matter of that, letter is the property of ether,[3] we can no longer maintain that letters form the constituents of words in view of the fact that attributes (*guṇa*-entities) have no title to be treated as the constitutive or the inherent cause (*samavāyi-kāraṇa*), a characteristic which invariably belongs to substances (*dravya*).[4]

Thereafter, Vācaspati turns to the school of philosophers who opine that letters are formed of the molecules of air[5] and that they are destroyed as soon as they are produced. That being so, it is argued by the grammarian that we can never speak of the co-existence of letters which are said to build up a particular word. Let us, for illustration, take up the word '*cow*' in which there are three letters. Now, it is never possible for us to pronounce all the three letters at one and the same time. And, as it is a fact that the first letter dies out before the third one is pronounced, the concept of word as an aggregate of letters is something fictitious for the obvious reason that there can be no combination of things that are not simultaneously present.

But, this position involves a further absurdity. The individual letters that perish after they are uttered and do not persist up to the time the final letter is pronounced, cannot be regarded either as the constitutive cause (*samavāyi-kāraṇa*) or as the proximate non-inherent cause (*asamavāyi-kāraṇa*) with regard to word. Now, the constitutive cause is one that enters into the composition of the product as a constituent factor. Or, to be precise, it is the persistent causal entity in which the effect is seen to inhere. And, the non-inherent cause is that which inheres in the causal entities and determines the effect though it does not enter into its composition. Letters, being momentary phenomena, cannot enter as componental factors into the constitution of word. Consequently, the question of their being the constitutive cause of word cannot arise. And, there being no co-existence among letters that are said to build up word, they cannot be supposed to be the bearer of a relation, which is usually the non-inherent cause. In the circumstances, word will be destitute of a constitutive and a non-inherent cause and in spite of the fact that it is a product, it cannot be subject to destruction.

Let us pursue the point in detail. It is an admitted fact that of the three causes contributing towards the production of an effect, it is the non-inherent cause which is the most proximate; and it is a truism that the destruction of a product is due to the disappearance of the non-inherent cause. If the disappearance of the inherent and not of the non-inherent cause be regarded as the cause of the destruction of a product, such entities as an 'aggregate of two atoms' (*dvyaṇuka*) would come under the category of eternal (*nitya*) entities. A *dvyaṇuka* is said to be formed of two atoms (*paramāṇu*) and as the latter are believed to possess an eternal character, they cannot be destroyed under any circumstances. That being so, *dvyaṇuka* will never admit of destruction. Hence, the Neo-logician maintains that it is the disappearance of the non-inherent or the proximate cause and not of the inherent one that leads to the destruction of a product. Thus, whenever the connection between the two *paramāṇus* constituting a particular *dvyaṇuka*, will be severed, the latter will cease to exist.[6]

To come to the point, it has been already stated that the several letters which are said to make up a word, are pronounced in succession and, so, the question of the non-inherent cause and consequently of its disappearance cannot arise. It is, therefore, that Vācaspati points out that we cannot conceive of the destruction of a word which is said to have been produced. And, to say that a thing has birth and no death is anything but a dogmatic statement.[7]

From what has been said above, it becomes clear that *conjointly* letters cannot express sense. And, it is quite obvious that they are incapable of expressing the required import *singly* as well; for, in that case, there will hardly be any justification for using a number of letters when any one of them is sufficient for the purpose.

The grammarian, thus, points out the outstanding difficulties for those who opine that letters are expressive of sense. And, in order to explain satisfactorily all the points at issue, they have, in their turn, propounded their own theory according to which sense is expressed by *sphoṭa* which in its character is indivisible and is revealed more and more distinctly by each one of the different sounds (or, different letters) in succession and finally and completely by the last sound (or, letter).[8]

We propose to discuss the merits of the theory in course of our subsequent disquisitions. But, before doing so, it is imperative on our part to examine the grounds of objection put forth by those who oppose the theory.

GROUNDS OF OBJECTION

Both the Mīmāṁsakas and the Naiyāyikas vehemently criticise the theory of *sphoṭa* on vital grounds. The *Śabara-bhāṣya* on the *Mīmāṁsāsūtra* I.i.5. makes it sufficiently clear that the theory of *sphoṭa* has been discarded by the Mīmāṁsakas on the ground that it strikes at the root of some of the fundamental principles of the system of their philosophy. It has been already remarked in a foregoing section that Bhartṛhari understands by *sphoṭa* an indivisible sentence which is expressive of sense. He has definitely stated that a word or letter has no reality by itself apart from that of a sentence. Following in his wake, the later grammarians of his school have said in unambiguous terms that *vākya-sphoṭa* is the only type of denoter (*vācaka*), and that other classifications of *sphoṭa* are mere artifices resorted to for the purpose of enabling the beginner to comprehend the sentence as a totality by itself.[9]

The Mīmāṁsakas point out that if word, in particular, be regarded as fictitious carrying no meaning of its own, such technical operations as *ūha*, *prasaṅga* and *tantra*,[10] which have been discussed at length in their system of thought, become absolutely meaningless.[11]

The Vedas sanction a change in the wording of a hymn according to a change of circumstances. While discussing the question—Are Vedic hymns intended to convey any meaning?—Sāyaṇa strongly maintains that the Vedic hymns are expressive of sense on the ground that it has been enjoined to make necessary changes in the wording in the case of a derivative sacrifice.[12]

It has been laid down in the *Taittirīya-brāhmaṇa* III. vi. 6. ii, that for purposes of a principal animal sacrifice, only one animal is sufficient and, hence, the hymn reads thus :— *anv enaṁ mātā manyatām anu pitā anu bhrātā.* But, in the case of a derivative sacrifice where two or more animals are required, the authorities sanction a change in the wording and the term '*enam*' (which is in the singular) is replaced by '*enau*' (i.e., the dual) or '*enān*' (i.e., the plural) as the case may be. It is why Śabara remarks that the injunction of the *Brāhmaṇa* — Neither '*pitā*' nor '*mātā*' should be increased (in the case of a derivative sacrifice), leads us to infer that the word '*enam*' is required to be increased and he explicitly states that this *increase* refers to an *increase* in sense as represented by a change in the forms of declension. Sāyaṇa says it in so many words that the singular in '*enaṃ*' should be replaced by the dual or the plural according to a change in meaning. That being so, it is established that every Vedic word has a meaning attached to it and the same is expressed through its power of denotation.

The exponents of the theory of *sphoṭa*, as we have already observed, believe that it is neither the word nor the letter but the indivisible sentence which is endowed with the power of expressing a coherent sense; and it is on this account that the Mīmāṁsakas cannot accept the theory of the grammarians.

THE GRAMMARIANS' REVIEW OF THE POSITION OF THE MĪMĀṀSAKAS

The grammarians point out that the Mīmāṁsakas have misunderstood the whole point. The grammarians' attitude towards word is twofold, viz., metaphysical or transcendental, empirical or practical. From the metaphysical point of view, the Ultimate Reality is the Absolute Word or *Śabda-brahman* as it is called, which is bereft of all distinctions and, is therefore, a homogeneous entity without a second, just like the *Brahman* of the Vedāntists so far as it is explained by Śaṅkarācārya. From the empirical point of view, this *Śabda-brahman* is susceptible of further and further divisions from *vākya-sphoṭa* down to *varṇa-sphoṭa*. There is, therefore, little ground for an apprehension on the part of the Mīmāṁsakas, as *vākya-sphoṭa* has obviously no title to be regarded as superior in merits to *pada-sphoṭa*, since both of them are fictitious divisions necessitated by the operation of *avidyā* to serve the practical purposes of our everyday life.

From what has been said above, it may appear to the casual student of Sanskrit Grammar that the position of Bhartṛhari cannot be satisfactorily explained, for he accords a place of honour to *vākya-sphoṭa* and does not attach much importance to *pada-sphoṭa* and *varṇa-sphoṭa*. It is for this reason that we propose to enter into an intensive study of the whole issue, so that the viewpoint of the grammarians be presented in its proper perspective and there be little room for any misunderstanding whatsoever.

From the empirical point of view, Bhartṛhari puts premium upon a complete self-contained proposition (*vākya*) as the unit of verbal usage which alone possesses the power of expressing a coherent sense capable of being turned into practical use. Letters and words do not independently possess this denotative capacity which is rather ascribed to them by virtue of their necessary contribution to the formation of propositions. Although Bhartṛhari seems to put words on the same level with letters, both being subservient to the constitution of propositions and, as such, they are relegated to the position of unmeaning expressions, it would be rather wide off the mark to suppose that words are pure nonsense like unmeaning sounds. The purpose of Bhartṛhari seems to be not to disparage the value of words but rather to emphasise the self-sufficiency of propositions as the minimum of linguistic usage. So, the Mīmāṁsakas have no reason to be alarmed, because even from their standpoint, words cannot be regarded as self-sufficient units of expression. Of course, contribution of words to the formation of propositions is not disregarded or denied even by the grammarians. But, it should always be carefully remembered that the grammarians have denied the transcendental validity of parts of speech as they are always parts and never wholes. So, even from the empirical standpoint, the status of parts of speech may be described as being lower than propositions which the Mīmāṁsakas, too, cannot deny. And, if the denial of transempirical validity be the ground of complaint, the grammarians would fain plead guilty. It has been proved ever and anon that such transcendental validity has no bearing upon our practical conduct which is satisfied by the empirical standard of validity.

MAṆḌANA'S VIEW

We have stated the position of the grammarians and we expect that the Mīmāṁsakas would not have any cause for apprehension. But, we should not stop here. We go a step further to mention that Maṇḍana-miśra, a great pioneer of the *Pūrva-mīmāṁsā* system, has said that there is absolutely no valid ground to deny the existence of *sphoṭa* as a spiritual entity. In his *Sphoṭa-siddhi*, he refutes the arguments of Kumārila who in his *Śloka-vārttika*, has tried to prove that there is hardly any necessity for the postulation of *sphoṭa*.[13] Maṇḍana carefully examines the views of the great master and finally establishes the doctrine of *sphoṭa*. And, it needs to be mentioned in this connection that though Maṇḍana has, in particular, discussed the nature of *pada-sphoṭa*, he has spoken of *vākya-sphoṭa* as well.[14] That being so, each word is shown to be significant and there is ample justification for a change in the wording of a hymn with a corresponding change in the meaning.

THE NAIYĀYIKAS AND THEIR OBJECTION

The Naiyāyikas also do not accept the grammarians' theory of *sphoṭa* for more reasons than one. Jayanta-bhaṭṭa clearly points out that it should not be supposed that the Naiyāyikas criticise the doctrine of *sphoṭa* only to make a parade of their power of argumentation. The theory of *sphoṭa* is opposed to the vital principles of their philosophy. The Naiyāyikas have established the authority of word (*śabda*) as a cognitive instrument (*pramāṇa*) by proving that it was created by God. We have pointed out that the grammarians describe word (*śabda*) as something eternal. And, as an entity which is said to be eternal cannot be created by any being, be it human or divine, the Naiyāyikas cannot but refuse to accept the theory of the grammarians.[15]

But the argument of the Naiyāyikas, as stated above, seems to be frivolous and the charge acts like a boomerang upon themselves. The Naiyāyikas make the validity of verbal knowledge (*śābda-bodha*) conditional on God whereas the grammarians and the Mīmāṁsakas make it a self-sufficient instrument of knowledge.

The Naiyāyikas, may, however, point out that word

(*śabda*) in their system of thought is regarded as possessing transient existence; it is said to be produced at one moment, exists for the next moment and dies out at the third moment. But, the grammarians conceive word as one endowed with a permanent character. Thus, the conception of word being different in the two systems of thought, the Naiyāyikas naturally raise a note of protest against the theory of *sphoṭa* as propounded by the grammarians.

THE NAIYĀYIKA VIEW : LETTERS AND NOT SPHOṬA EXPRESS SENSE

The Naiyāyikas observe a relation of agreement in presence and absence between perception of letters and cognition of sense; and it is for this reason that the two are described to be causally related.[16] They maintain that with the perception of letters we understand some sense and that the cognition of sense cannot proceed without the perception of letters. It is, therefore, reasonable to admit that letters are endowed with the power of expressing sense; and to posit a transcendental entity, viz., *sphoṭa*, for this purpose is hardly warranted. The Naiyāyikas again, point out to their advantage that letters are designated as *śabda* (word) for the only reason that they are perceived by the auditory organ.[17] *Sphoṭa*, on the contrary, can be cognised only through mental perception.[18] It has been said that the realisation of *sphoṭa* requires a mental discipline and spiritual meditation. Hence, the Naiyāyikas opine that when *sphoṭa* is not perceived in the usual course, it is certainly desirable that letters which are ordinarily perceived, should be regarded as denotative of meaning. Thus, when verbal knowledge (*śābda-bodha*) can be easily explained as accruing from the perception of letters, the Naiyāyikas do not find any justification for postulating a spiritual entity like *sphoṭa* as causing the cognition of meaning.

THE GRAMMARIANS' REPLY TO THE NAIYĀYIKAS

The grammarians, however, criticise the view of the Naiyāyikas on this point. They maintain that the arguments of opponents are based on flimsy grounds. With the help of a dilemmatic argument, they point out the weakness to which the Naiyāyika theory is exposed. Do letters *singly* or *conjointly* express sense ? — ask they. Evidently, the first alternative is untenable. If the second alternative be accepted, a question may be put further : is it required to have an aggregate of letters alone or is the cognition of that aggregate also compulsory ?

It should be noted that the Naiyāyikas cannot contemplate such an aggregate on the ground that each letter is transient and not permanent. It may be argued, of course, that as, according to the Mīmāṁsakas who follow Upavarṣa of respectable fame and antiquity, letters are not supposed to be perishable in character, they are not destroyed as soon as they are pronounced, an aggregate of letters may be logically comprehensible. But, before we criticise this point, we intend to examine the views of Upavarṣa regarding the permanent character of letters.

UPAVARṢA'S CONCEPTION OF LETTERS

Vācaspati in his *Bhāmatī*, the celebrated commentary on the *Śārīraka-bhāṣya* of Śaṅkarācārya, explains the position of this school by asserting that there is no authority to substantiate the truth of the proposition that letters are perishable and have momentary existence. The *Śārīraka-bhāṣya* has the most important observation on this point. Letters are not of a momentary character on the ground that at the time of recognition (*pratyabhijñā*), they are recognised not as something *similar* to what have been previously perceived but as *identical* with them. The *Bhāmatī* clearly puts it that even when we utter the word 'cow' for a thousand and one times, we do not perceive that the word on each occasion is a different one and that each closely resembles the other. On the contrary, we perceive that the same word is pronounced on each occasion. But, when we observe one cow after another, we never say that the second animal is the same as the first. What we say is that the second one is something similar to the first. It is exactly for this reason that Upavarṣa maintains that when a letter pronounced at different times is not different in character, there is absolutely little justification for the assumption that it is transient.[19]

CRITICISM OF UPAVARṢA'S CONCEPTION OF LETTERS

Let us, now, point out the difficulties, that make their appearance in the event of the supposition that letters, which are said to have permanent character, are expressive of sense. In the first place, when all letters are permanent, it is difficult to ascertain which particular sense is expressed by which particular group of letters. Secondly, we cannot speak of the sequence of letters with reference to either time or space in view of the supposition that they are eternal entities. Letters are regarded by the Mīmāṁsakas as all-pervasive like space and, as such, it is inconceivable how there can be any sequence, temporal or spatial, between letters.

As for the problem whether the aggregate of letters is required to be known prior to verbal cognition, a few words are necessary by way of clarification. In all cases of perceptual knowledge (*pratyakṣa*), it is necessary that the sense-organ comes into contact with the object to be perceived. A jar, for instance, is said to be perceived when the eye falls upon it or the hand feels it. It should be carefully noted that besides the contact between the sense-organ and the object, the cognition of the sense-organ is not needed in a case of perceptual knowledge. But, in all cases of mediate knowledge (*parokṣa*), the causes must be known by themselves and in relation to their parts. For instance, in the case of an inferential knowledge, the *probans* itself is required to be known and also that it is invariably concomitant with the major term (*sādhya-vyāpya*). In the time-honoured example of inference in Hindu Logic, viz., 'There is fire on the top of the mountain because there is smoke' (*parvato bahnimān dhūmāt*), we may observe that before we are able to draw the inference we should be possessed of the knowledge of smoke (i.e., the probans), of the invariable concomitance (*vyāpti*) between smoke and fire (i.e., the major term) and the like.

To come to the point, verbal knowledge (*śābda-bodha*) being a case of mediate knowledge, it is required that we should also have a perception of both letters and their aggregate before any verbal knowledge is obtained. Thus, the cognition of an aggregate of letters becomes a necessity for purposes of verbal knowledge and it is to be seen whether such a cognition is logically possible.

It has been maintained that the conception of an aggregate of letters is not altogether impossible provided the different letters are pronounced by different persons all at one and the same time. It should, however, be pointed out that, though an aggregate of letters may be contemplated in this way, the cognition of that aggregate cannot be obtained. For, when several persons speak at a time there is a confused noise and, as such, it is quite impossible to understand which particular letters have been pronounced. But, even granting for argument's sake that one is competent to comprehend the different sounds simultaneously as pronounced by different persons at the same moment, it is never given in experience that such an aggregate of letters does express any sense.[20] And, if it be maintained that the letters will be pronounced by one man, it is obvious that each letter will have to be uttered at successive moments of time; for, to be pronounced different letters require different efforts and consequently an aggregate is out of question and, further still, is the knowledge of the same.[21]

2. *A Critique of the Objections from the Nyāya and Mīmāṁsā Schools*—Continued.

LOGICAL OBJECTIONS RAISED BY THE GRAMMARIANS

It has been argued by the Mīmāṁsakas and the Naiyāyikas that though letters cannot express sense either singly or conjointly, it may be legitimately supposed that the cognition of the final letter in a word accompanied by the memory-impressions (*saṁskāra*) produced by the perception of the preceding letters, is capable of expressing the required sense.[22]

But, this view is open to serious logical objections. It is admitted on all hands that the nature of impression is such that a particular impression caused by the perception of a particular object, is endowed with the power of reviving the same object to our memory and nothing else. That being an established fact, it is only natural that the impressions of letters are capable of reviving letters to our memory and it is not expected that they will express import as well.[23]

To say, therefore, that these impressions are competent to function that way is tantamount to denying an admitted fact. But, Kumārila still maintains that nobody disputes the fact that unless there lie in us the impressions of letters already perceived, we cannot remember the import and it is, therefore, reasonable to posit that impressions may be expressive of sense. He, therefore, sees no reason why the services of a new spiritual entity like *sphoṭa* should be requisitioned.

MAṆḌANA CRITICISES KUMĀRILA

Maṇḍana opines that impression, which is regarded as a power (*śakti*) itself, cannot be supposed to be endowed with another power (*śakti*). Parameśvara, the author of *Gopālikā*, a commentary on Maṇḍana's *Sphoṭa-siddhi*, explains the point by saying that impression should be looked upon either as a power of previous cognitions residing in the soul or a power of the soul and emanating from previous cognitions.[24] But, if this power be supposed to be possessed of another power, the latter, in its turn, may be similarly supposed to be possessed of another again, and the process continuing, there will be no limit to our suppositions.[25]

CRITICISM OF MAṆḌANA'S VIEWPOINT

It should be clearly pointed out that the arguments advanced by Maṇḍana are not very sound. It is a fact that we find that the cognition of import proceeds from impressions arising out of the cognitions of letters and it becomes necessary, therefore, to admit that impressions are endowed with the power of expressing sense. But, when we do not find that this power has any other operation (*kārya*) to perform, there is absolutely no scope for the apprehension that, this power being endowed with another, there will be no limit to our suppositions. To be explicit, a power is admitted in order to explain any particular effect and when such an effect is not forthcoming, the question of the supposition of power does not arise at all.

Maṇḍana in all probability saw through the weakness of his own position and it is, therefore, that he says that the arguments of his adversary who admits the power of impressions to express import, seem to be based on flimsy grounds.[26] Thus, he hints at the fact that impressions may be supposed to be endowed with the power of giving us the cognition of import.

Śrīdhara in his *Nyāya-kandalī* has criticised the position of Maṇḍana so far as this particular point is concerned. He says that there is hardly any authority to say that impressions cannot express import. And, he states that it is certainly more economical to posit that impressions are capable of expressing meaning than to admit *sphoṭa* and its power of denotation as well.[27]

It may be further added that it is the Mīmāṁsakas who admit impression to be a power (*śakti*); but the Naiyāyikas regard the same as an attribute (*guṇa*). That being so, Maṇḍana's objection that the position of the Mīmāṁsakas involves *regression* is quite inconsequential with regard to the Naiyāyikas. It is only for this reason that Maṇḍana starts a new line of criticism. He drags in the question of *sequence* or *order* (*krama*) and points out that in the case of words having the same letters but in different orders, we cannot explain the difference in meaning, as there is nothing to prove that impressions arising out of identical letters are different in their nature.[28]

CRITICISM OF THE VIEW OF THE MĪMĀṀSAKAS AND THE NAIYĀYIKAS

The explanation offered by the Mīmāṁsakas and the Naiyāyikas that the auditory perception of the final letter reinforced by memory-impressions of previous letters results in the idea of one unitary word which is expressive of sense, appears to be a farfetched hypothesis. For, there is no such instance on the analogy of which, this explanation could be accepted. The case of recognition in which a particular sense-organ as assisted by previous memory-impressions produces a judgment of identity, stands altogether in a different category. Because, the resultant knowledge is but a judgment in which the identity of a present datum with a past datum is cognised; but, in the case of word-cognition, the resultant knowledge, supposed to be produced by the auditory organ aided by memory-impressions of previous letters, is a simple cognition and not a judgment of relations. So, the analogy of recognition is absolutely irrelevant to the present case.

IMPRESSIONS EXPRESS SENSE THROUGH THE MEDIUM OF RECOLLECTION

But, it has been contended that impressions will not directly express sense but will serve the purpose through the medium of recollection (*smṛti*).[29] To be explicit, sense will be expressed by the final letter which is perceived together with the preceding letters that are recollected.

It may be pointed out that this policy of shifting the ground has proved to be of little avail. It will be a fair question to ask whether the last letter will be perceived at the same time when preceding letters are recollected or whether the recollection of preceding letters will follow the perception of the last letter. And, it may be pointed out that either of the alternatives is not a safe plank to take one's stand upon. If it be maintained that the perception and the recollection happen at one and the same time, we may be permitted to mention that this leads us to admit a concurrence of cognitions at their birth (*jñāna-yaugapadya*); and, we all know that such a concurrence of cognitions is hardly accepted by philosophers. If it be maintained, on the other hand, that the said recollection will follow the perception of the final letter, the question of sequence comes in once again and, with it, all the difficulties standing in the way of obtaining an aggregate of letters. We may further point out that even if preceding letters are recollected, there is no reason why they will be recollected in the same order in which they are perceived.[30] Vācaspati states it clearly that it may be assumed that the recollected letters are expressive of sense but there is hardly any justification for the assumption that they will be recollected only in the same order in which they have been perceived before; for, they may as well be recollected in a different order. The *Śārīraka-bhāṣya* while describing the grammarians' point of view, says that under the circumstances, such words as '*jārā*' and '*rājā*'[31] or '*kapi*' and '*pika*' will denote one and the same thing. But, when in the two cases cited above, we notice the same letters but find a difference in meaning, it has to be admitted that something besides letters expresses sense; and, if this is once conceded, we have practically no difficulty in establishing a case for *sphoṭa*.

But, let us turn to see how our opponents propose further modifications of their hypothesis which we have been criticising so long. In order to obviate the difficulty, it has been proposed that different impressions resulting from separate cognitions of various letters in succession will give rise to *one single recollection* and all the letters that have been cognised before will flash in the mirror of this recollection; and, because the successive letters can thus be collectively recollected at one and the same time, it will enable us to affirm the co-existence of letters and to uphold that these letters may be looked upon as expressive of sense.[32]

a *tertium quid* in the shape of *sphoṭa* and there is no economy in the assumption of causal conditions. To be explicit, first of all, there is the perception of word or sound; secondly, the cognition of *sphoṭa* and thirdly, the comprehension of meaning. But, this is exactly the position of the Naiyāyikas and the Mīmāṁsakas, only with this exception that recollection is substituted for *sphoṭa*. The contention of the Naiyāyikas and the Mīmāṁsakas is quite plausible. But, it seems that the grammarians have this advantage over the Naiyāyikas and the Mīmāṁsakas that their theory has the sanction of experience. *Sphoṭa* is a perceived fact and from this, meaning is understood. And, such is the testimony of our introspective experience too. The hypothesis of the Naiyāyikas and the Mīmāṁsakas is absolutely destitute of this sanction of experience. It is never felt by us whenever a word is heard that there is the recollection of a word or of letters.

Furthermore, this collective recollection is subject to the same limitations to which all recollections are liable. For instance, a recollection is only a reproduction of a previous perceptual knowledge and is never credited with the capacity for giving us any new information which was not known before. So, collective recollection is only possible if there is a collective perception behind it. And, if a collective perception is admitted, the hypothesis of collective recollection would be absolutely futile; for, the former would give us the knowledge of the word for which the latter hypothesis was requisitioned.

JAYANTA'S EXPLANATION AND ITS CRITICISM

Jayanta, the astute Naiyāyika, was shrewd enough to perceive the drawbacks in the previous theory and, so, he comes forward with another hypothesis. The resultant cognition of an entire word is not regarded as recollection but rather as a mental judgment. Jayanta contends that though the different cognitions of constituent letters occur successively and, as such, letters are never perceived together, still a cognition of totality is not impossible as in the judgment that 'Devadatta has eaten a hundred fruits,'[33] the successive consumptions of different fruits are synthesised in one judgment. So, also in the case of letters, a synthetic judgment comprising within its scope the successive presentation of letters and thus giving us the knowledge of the unitary whole is not at all an impossible phenomenon. If, on the contrary, such mental judgments are declared to be impossible on the ground of the successive presentation of the data, all our activities resulting from such judgment will be reduced to an impossibility and the synthetic unity of our personal conscious life, which is being continuously enriched by the contributions of our past and present experiences, will be impossible.

While admiring the philosophical insight of Jayanta, we cannot help thinking that Jayanta has been led by specious similarities and the cases cited by him as precedents are absolutely without any bearing on the issue. The knowledge of a number, say, a hundred, is only a memory-judgment at bottom. Or, if it is regarded as a new intellectual judgment as the knowledge of the number was not given in the individual perceptions, still, the analogy of such judgments with the simple experience of word-units is not at all patent to our understanding. The knowledge of the number is after all a synthetic construction and not a simple presentation, and it is made possible by the knowledge of relations of constituent units. The content of such a judgment is not a simple unity but rather a group-concept in which the different individuals are comprised in one group with their distinctive individualities unimpaired. But, the cognition of word-units is not a case of group-conception. It is, on the contrary, a simple apprehension of a simple identity without any reference whatsoever to its individual constituents, the existence of which is simply uncognised. The analogy could hold good if our cognitions of word-units were conversant with the presence of the different letters as constituent factors. When I judge that I have eaten a hundred fruits, this judgment though unitary in character, does not annul the separate cognitions of the different fruits that have been consumed. But, when I say that Devadatta is the name of a person, I am not at all aware of the fact that the name 'Devadatta' is a collection of letters. My experience, on the contrary, is that the word 'Devadatta' is a simple unit. The whole argument of Jayanta, therefore, seems to be based upon superficial similarities and far-fetched constructions designed to vindicate a weak case for which there is no support from experience. Jayanta seems to have been conscious of the weakness of his position and, therefore, gives his blessings to the theory of Śabara, namely, that the final letter together with the memory-impressions of previous letters produces a direct cognition of meaning.[34] The implication of this theory of Śabara, as we have fully discussed before, is that memory-impressions though generally productive of recollection, may produce a direct cognition as well.

The whole pleadings of Jayanta are, no doubt, admirable for their ingenuity; but, we must admit that they have failed to carry conviction. We have exposed the defects of his theory of synthetic cognition and this theory, too, does not stand a better chance. Why should Jayanta go out of his way to put so much power to the credit of memory-impressions? Its purpose is obvious; namely, to refute the doctrine of *sphoṭa* for which he has no patience. This is altogether an unwarranted assumption to suppose that memory-impressions can achieve the impossible task of giving us a direct cognition of a simple unity though that unity is not in existence. Jayanta in his zeal against his opponents forgot to take notice of the consequences of his theory. The theory makes the knowledge of words and sentences a case of unmitigated illusion. The plurality of letters is believed to be a simple unity which it is not. Certainly, there is no logical necessity to suppose that our cognitions of word-units or sentence-units as simple unities are false cognitions.

Likewise, the possible contention of the Neo-logicians that previous letters may be present through their cognitions or that memory-impressions and that these, together with the final letter, may result in the cognition of a word-unit, is not reasonable. Because, the presentation through cognition which is called *jñānalakṣaṇā-sannikarṣa* is not universally accepted; and, even according to the Naiyāyikas' theory, it is not found to result in the knowledge of a simple unity, but rather in a complex judgment, the presented data through such cognition being added as adjectival elements as in the judgment — 'I see a fragrant piece of sandal-wood.' And, so the Naiyāyikas' explanations are found to be at variance with their accepted conclusions and this shows more zeal than logic.

Moreover, Jayanta does not make any economy. As we had occasion to remark before, *sphoṭa* is dispensed with only to make room for an intermediate condition, viz., memory-impression or memory. Jayanta is obviously under the illusion that the upholders of *sphoṭa* assume all these conditions and *sphoṭa* as an additional category. But, this is not the case. The *sphoṭa-vādins* need not assume the existence of memory-impressions as the condition of the perception of *sphoṭa.* Individual letters successively reveal the same *sphoṭa* and this revelation becomes more and more decisive and clear, the final letter resulting in the complete revelation of *sphoṭa.*

MAṆḌANA'S REVIEW OF THE POSITION OF THE NAIYĀYIKAS AND THE MĪMĀṀSAKAS

We cannot close this section without referring to the views of Maṇḍana on this particular point. Maṇḍana has recorded no less than three different views of his opponents as to how the import is obtained. In the first place, he states that the different cognitions of different letters will give rise to different impressions which will enable letters to flash in one single recollection in the same order in which they have been perceived. Next, he refers to the view according to which a single cognition, in which the last letter will be cognised and the preceding ones recollected in the same order in which they have been perceived, will be the medium through which letters will express the required sense. And, the third view is that there arises one recollection immediately after the cognition of the last letter, and in this recollection flash all the preceding letters in the same order in which they have been perceived.[35] Thus, on the second moment of the cognition of the last letter we have the recollection. And, as there is no bar to the simultaneous existence of two cognitions, there is absolutely no possibility of any difficulty making its appearance. Maṇḍana, however, remarks that of these three views it is the last one that is generally accepted by the opponents.

Before we pass on to see how Maṇḍana criticises the three views cited above, we should do well to discuss the niceties of distinction between the first view and the third. It is a fact that Maṇḍana's own language is not as clear and lucid as it should have been in order that we may form a correct and precise idea of his viewpoint and it is also unfortunate that the commentator, Parameśvara, does not give us any satisfactory explanation. We, therefore, propose to study the views independently of ourselves so that the real position may be fairly understood.

According to the first view, the single recollection happens only when we have the impressions of all the different letters in us. But, it has been discussed before that the impression of the final letter can only arise when the perception of the same has died out. So, the recollection supposed happens long after the perception of all the letters. It is for this reason that the attempt has been made to show that the recollection does not happen at a long interval — it happens on the second moment of the perception of the final letter. And, this is exactly the position in the third view.[36] Now, it may be argued that the impression of the last letter which also contributes to the birth of the recollection cannot be obtained on the second moment of the perception of the final letter. For, it is a general rule that the cause precedes the effect; and the impression which is said to be caused by the perception, cannot come into being simultaneously with the latter. But, we may point out that the above rule does not always hold good. In a case of perceptual knowledge we find that the object which is said to be the cause of its perception is designated as such only with reference to its simultaneous existence with the perception. Similarly, the perception of the final letter is the cause of the impression only in this way that the two exist simultaneously—there is no question of sequence. Thus, it will not be difficult for us to obtain the recollection on the second moment of the perception of the final letter.

Maṇḍana draws our pointed attention to the fact that in all the three views we find that the letters flash in the subsequent recollection or cognition exactly in the same order in which they are perceived. And, it seems, therefore, that the opponents want to make their positions particularly safe by incorporating this fact in the exposition and explanation of their particular theories on verbal cognition (*śābda-bodha*). Maṇḍana criticises all the three views and his criticism is mainly directed along the following channel. There is practically nothing in favour of his opponents to maintain that letters will invariably be recollected or cognised in the same order in which they are perceived. For, he firmly asserts that the previous perceptions which have died out, cannot in any way effect any distinction with regard to the letters that have not come into existence. And, he has made it sufficiently clear on more occasions than one that there is no difference in nature between what has not come to pass and what has happened but had died out without leaving any trace behind.[37] Furthermore, we are hardly justified in bringing in the notion of sequence in a unitary recollection. For, sequence or order invariably implies distinction (*bheda*). And, when the recollection that is posited is a unified whole, the question of sequence cannot arise in this case as unity and distinction are contradictory in nature and we can hardly speak of them in the same breath with reference to one and the same identity.[38] It is only when the notion of distinction has completely vanished that we are in a position to have the recollection that 'cow', for instance, is one word. Thus, Maṇḍana deals a staggering blow to the theory of the Naiyāyikas who have been maintaining that the sequence of letters will also appear in the recollection. The Mīmāṁsakas, too, cannot raise the question of sequence at all; for, according to them, letters are eternal and ubiquitous and there cannot be any sequence, temporal or spatial, between letters.[39]

Thus, we conclude that we cannot conceive of any one collective cognition — be it in the nature of one in which we have all the letters recollected or the last one perceived and the rest recollected —in which we have all the letters at one and the same time and also in the order in which they are successively perceived.

KUMĀRILA'S SOLUTION

Kumārila in his *Śloka-vārttika* has in all probability anticipated the difficulties mentioned above and has attempted to steer clear of the same. He argues that the sense which a particular word is found to express is determined by usage — that is, how it has been practically used and understood; and, as such, the particular number of letters uttered by one individual and in a particular order too, which has expressed the import to us when we have first learnt the word from our elders will express the same sense at all future times.[40] And, Kumārila believes that this explanation is quite sufficient to put an end to all the difficulties raised heretofore.

MAṆḌANA CRITICISES KUMĀRILA

Maṇḍana carefully summarises the viewpoint of Kumārila and he opines that according to Kumārila, it is letters that are endowed with the power of denotation; but, these letters should be understood not in their absolute but qualified character. It is why, says Maṇḍana, Kumārila posits that letters as found in traditional usage will express the required import. But, Maṇḍana points out that this explanation does not improve the position in any way. For, the question that still remains to be decided is whether such letters will be expressive of sense singly or conjointly. And, Maṇḍana maintains that in order to decide the problem, we shall be once more required to cover the same ground hitherto traversed.

We prefer to criticise Kumārila in a different way. The apprehension of the import of a word depends upon how our elders have understood the same. But, it is not possible for us to know how the import of a particular word has been understood by our elders. In that case it is only necessary to point out that this explanation of Kumārila only seeks to evade an obvious difficulty. Kumārila lays stress upon the number and the order of letters in a word and puts the expressive power to their credit. But, we have seen that this order cannot be substantiated by argument. Order is ultimately a question of sequence and this sequence could be realised if preceding, letters or their cognitions could be shown to be coincident or synchronous with subsequent letters and their cognitions. Preceding letters or their cognitions have completely died out without leaving any legacy behind and subsequent letters have not yet come into existence. So, there can be no co-operation among them. And, bereft of mutual co-operation, letters or cognitions are to be treated as isolated facts without any additional efficiency that may be supposed to be derived from mutual assistance. The extinction of preceding cognitions and the non-production of succeeding cognitions are both equally cases of non-existence and non-existent facts cannot be supposed to have any efficacy. The difficulty may be obviated by the supposition of the presence of legacies in the shape of memory-impressions; but, we have weighed them in the scale and found them to be wanting in the efficiency sought to be put to their credit.

3. *The Grammarians' Theory and its Advantages*

THEORY OF SPHOṬA INVOLVES NO DIFFICULTY

It is for this reason that the grammarians point out that when the theory that letters are expressive of sense involves a lot of complications, a better and more satisfactory solution should, by all means, be found out. The grammarians, therefore, engage themselves in an intensive study of the problem and finally assert that it is *sphoṭa* which is really endowed with the power of denotation. And, they describe *sphoṭa* as an indivisible unit having an eternal existence gradually revealed by the articulation of letters. From the trend of discussion, it has become quite clear that it is the problem of sequence which has practically dealt a staggering blow to the theory of the Naiyāyikas and the Mīmāṁsakas according to which letters are said to be expressive of sense. But, when the grammarians describe *sphoṭa* as an indivisible entity, all the difficulties lying that way are removed once for all.

THE THEORY HAS THE SANCTION OF USAGE

The grammarians point out that the indivisible character of *sphoṭa*, as conceived by them, is warranted by various linguistic expressions. They assert that the term 'word' (*śabda*) refers to *sphoṭa* and not to letters. It is a known fact that in such expressions as 'We learn the import from the word' (*śabdād arthaṁ pratipadyāmahe*) the singular number in the term 'word' can only be justified provided the said term means *sphoṭa* which is one and indivisible. But, if letters were signified by the said term, there would have been little justification for the use of the singular number instead of the plural. Besides, it is argued by the grammarians that such expressions as 'We learn the import from letters' (*varṇebhyo'rthaṁ pratipadyāmahe*) are not current. Moreover, the respective imports of the stem and the suffix need not be modified, provided the term 'word' means the indivisible *sphoṭa* and not letters. They further point out that the Naiyāyikas regard the term 'word' as one denotative of the class (*jāti-vācaka*). But, we know that when a word denotative of the class is used in apposition with a word denotative of the individual (*vyakti-vācaka*), the former cannot be used in the singular number if the latter be used in the dual or the plural. This being an established fact, the term '*śabdāt*' ought to have been replaced by the term '*śabdebhyaḥ*'. We may observe, for instance, that such expressions as 'Yajñadatta and Devadatta are a man,' or 'Dhava, Khadira and Palāśa are a tree' are nowhere to be found in use.[41] Similarly, we do not come across such an expression as 'c' 'o' and 'w' are a word.

The Naiyāyikas realise the weakness of their position and, so, they shift their ground and maintain that the term 'word' is not denotative of the class but of the whole (*samudāya*). And, they opine that in the case of two words, one of which is denotative of parts (*avayava-vācaka*) and the other denotative of the whole, it is not uncommon that the two show a difference in number when they are used in apposition. Thus, for instance, such expressions as 'The forest is trees' (*vanaṁ vṛkṣāḥ*) are not infrequent. But, we shall show that the Naiyāyikas cannot carry their point even now. It should be carefully noted that in the case of two words, one of which is denotative of the part and the other of whole, we may use them either in apposition or in their natural relation. Thus, we often use such expressions as 'The forest of mango trees' (*āmrāṇāṁ vanam*), 'The forest of wood-apple trees' (*kapitthānāṁ vanam*), etc. But, do we ever come across such expressions as 'The word of c, o and w' ? It is, therefore, that we cannot say that the term 'word' is denotative of the whole (*samudāya-vācaka*).

We should not, however, stop here but enter into a detailed discussion of the point at issue. In the case of such terms as 'forest' and 'tree', there is a marked difference between the part (i.e., tree) and the whole (i.e., forest), because the latter cannot be predicated of each one of the parts which go to constitute it; and so, in such cases we may be permitted to imagine the relation of apposition subsisting between the two. But, the difference between word and letters cannot be conceived and, so, the supposition of identity is absolutely out of question. Thus, we conclude that word is not an entity which is denotative of the whole. And, we have already proved that word is not denotative of the class too. This is how the grammarians expose the weakness of the Naiyāyika theory.

HOW TO EXPLAIN THE UNITY OF WORD ?

The grammarians again raise another subtle and interesting point. It is said that the oneness pertaining to word is an established fact. But, the difficulty crops up when the Naiyāyikas are asked to explain the same. Jayanta takes up the discussion and says that the cognition of oneness pertaining to word is not natural but due to foreign association (*aupādhika*). Thus, he maintains that the oneness pertaining to the cognition of the import of a word is reflected, as it were, in the cognition of the word itself. But, the grammarians point out that the aforesaid exposition involves a fallacy of reasoning. For, it is a fact that the cognition of the unity of a word is regarded as the cause of the unity of the cognition of the import of a word; and to say that the latter is the cause of the former is liable to involve interdependence. But, the Naiyāyikas argue that it is the aggregate of letters, the last one of which is perceived and the rest recollected, that should be regarded as the cause of the oneness pertaining to the cognition of the import of the word; and thus, they appear to steer clear of the difficulty. But, the grammarians point out that it is the *oneness* pertaining to the word that determines the oneness pertaining to the cognition of the import. Jayanta, however, says that the oneness pertaining to the cognition of the import of a word presupposes the oneness of the import which is the matter (*viṣaya*) of the cognition and not of the word which is instrumental in effecting the same. For, he asserts that the oneness or otherwise pertaining to the cognition implies the corresponding oneness or otherwise pertaining to the matter of cognition and not to the instruments (*upāya*).[42] Jayanta explains his point by means of an illustration. He says that in the case of perception, there are more than one instrument of cognition, e.g., the eye, adequate light, the mind and others. But, all these instruments certainly enable us to obtain one cognition. Thus, when we perceive a pot, the matter of perception being one, we are said to have one cognition and not *many*.

CRITICISM OF JAYANTA'S EXPLANATION

But, may we criticise Jayanta in the following way? It may be pointed out that when the finger presses against the eyeball we find that the object which is really one, appears to be many in view of the fact that the instrument of perception, viz., the eye, is not one at that time; the eye being pressed, is divided into several sections and, so, we do not obtain one perception only but more. Moreover, the illustration which Jayanta cites is not well-chosen. According to Jayanta, there is a plurality of instruments in the case of perception. But, may we point out that in the aforesaid example, there is only one instrument of perception, and that is the eye, the rest being regarded as auxiliary (*sahakārin*) of it. Further, it is not proper to say that the oneness pertaining to the cognition of the import of the word presupposes only the oneness pertaining to the import on the ground that the same matter can be cognised by means of both perceptual and non-perceptual knowledge. And, in that case, it is the instrument of cognition that settles whether the cognition is perceptual or non-perceptual. Hence, the unity of the word is also of necessity presupposed by the unity pertaining to the cognition of the import of the word.

THE GRAMMARIANS' CRITICISM OF THE NAIYĀYIKAS' CONCEPTION OF WORD

The grammarians further criticise the view of the Naiyāyikas according to whom word (*śabda*) is used to refer to what is perceived by the auditory organ; and letters, being perceived through the auditory organ, can rightly be called word. According to Jayanta's exposition of the grammarians' viewpoint, *sphoṭa* is apprehended through the auditory organ;[43] and, as such, it is entitled to the designation of word. But, we have discussed before that the grammarians do not maintain that the auditory perception of *sphoṭa* is possible. So, they state their own conception of word and criticise the aforesaid view of the Naiyāyikas.

The grammarians aver that the Naiyāyikas have got to admit that like 'word', 'wordness', too, is cognised through the auditory organ; and that being so, the murmur of the wind or the splash of the wave is entitled to be designated as word. But, we may point out that such sounds are not included in the category of word on the ground that they do not express any sense. Hence, the grammarians conclude that the Naiyāyikas conception of word is not at all satisfactory.

The Naiyāyikas, however, do not drop the controversy here. They in their turn criticise the definition of word as set forth by Patañjali and say that the definition is wide[44] and not strictly scientific. According to Patañjali, word is that which is expressive of sense.[45] Now, the Naiyāyikas point out that if anything that expresses meaning be regarded as word, the *probans* in a piece of inferential knowledge has a right to be called such. When we, for instance, infer the existence of the fire on the hill-top from the sight of the smoke, we may be logically justified in drawing the conclusion that the smoke (which is really an object) is a word inasmuch as it enables us to obtain the knowledge of the fire.

The Naiyāyikas further point out that if word be defined as one which is expressive of sense, the difficulty arises that word cannot be designated as such unless it is known to be expressive of sense. Thus, prior to our knowledge of the fact that a particular word is expressive of a particular sense, it cannot be logically described as such and it is only when we have come to know that the sense is conveyed by it that we shall be justified in calling it a word. Thus, we find that one and the same thing happens to be a 'word' and also not it—a position which hardly commends itself to our reason.[46]

The grammarians, however, point out that the charges levelled against their theory cannot be substantiated in any way. At the outset, let us point out that the Naiyāyikas and the Mīmāṁsakas, too, have thoroughly misunderstood Patañjali's standpoint. Patañjali argues that as the word 'cow' is uttered or heard, various ideas present themselves to our mind;[47] but, can any one of them be taken up to explain what forms the word-element in the word 'cow' as contradistinguished from the sense-element ? Hence, it is that Kaiyaṭa clearly explains the implication of the query — '*atha gaur ity atra kaś śabdaḥ* ?' by saying that word and sense being identically used, it is necessary that the meaning of the word-element should be explicitly stated in the beginning of a treatise on the Science of Grammar. The word 'cow' is found to denote the dewlap, the tail, the hoofs and the horns of the animal; but, Patañjali is careful enough to point out that all of these form the sense-element on the ground that each of them is a substance (*dravya*) and not a word.[48] Kaiyaṭa explicitly states that each one of the substances, the dewlap, the hump, etc. referred to above, may be cognised by means of different cognitive instruments (*pramāṇa*) other than the auditory organ; and, as such, none can be regarded as word.[49] Having dismissed the claims of substances to be called word, Patañjali on selfsame grounds states that neither action (*kriyā*), nor attribute (*guṇa*), nor even configuration (*ākṛti*) can come under the scope of the word-element.[50] We may, therefore, conclude that according to Patañjali, word is one of those that can be cognised through the auditory organ but is expressive of sense. And, this definition does not apply to the logical probans in a syllogism.

Maṇḍana also observes that the Naiyāyikas and the Mīmāṁsakas have failed to understand the viewpoint of Patañjali; and, he explains his point by means of an apt illustration. Suppose there are several men in a room and Devadatta is one of them. Now, if we are asked to point out Devadatta, it is evidently meant that we are required to find him out from amongst his companions in the room and not from other objects, we mean, the different articles of furniture there. Similarly, when word has been defined as one endowed with the expressive power, it is understood that whatsoever happens to be expressive of sense is not word. On the contrary, what is meant as word is only a particular class of things that are apprehended through the auditory organ and not anything that is meant by it. It may mean the class (*jāti*), the individual (*vyakti*), action (*kriyā*), attribute (*guṇa*), letter (*varṇa*), *sphoṭa* and the like and these are meant by it as things distinct from it — as the expressed or suggested meaning in contradistinction to what it is in and by itself. So, there is no ambiguity in the meaning of word itself. Word is, therefore, regarded as self-meaning and this is evident from the query, "What is the word ?" The meaning of the term 'word' is here something in which what expresses the meaning is also included in what is expressed by it. It is, as it were, by an act of self-alienation that the same thing is regarded as the subject and the object both at the same time. Bhartṛhari is emphatic on this point of the self-expressive character of word. The Naiyāyikas and the Mīmāṁsakas only make themselves ridiculous by raising a quibble which is altogether out of place.[51]

CAUSAL RELATION BETWEEN PERCEPTION OF LETTERS AND COGNITION OF SENSE CANNOT BE PROVED

The grammarians, next, point out that the causal relation which the Naiyāyikas seek to establish between the perception of letters and the cognition of sense, is totally untenable. The Naiyāyikas prove that the cognition of sense is invariably preceded by the perception of letters and, as such, the former can be regarded as the effect of the latter. But, it should be noted that mere invariable sequence cannot establish causation. Mill states : "Invariable sequence, therefore, is not synonymous with causation, unless the sequence, besides being invariable, is unconditional. There are sequences, as uniform in past experience as any others whatever, which we yet do not regard as cases of causation, but as conjunctions in some sort accidental. Such to an accurate thinker is that of day and night."[52] Indian logicians have also made similar observations on this point when they define a cause as an invariable antecedent, which is not *anyathāsiddha* (irrelevant).[53]

To come to the point, we may show that the perception of letters is not the unconditional antecedent of the cognition of sense. For, it is with the perception of each one of the successive letters that *sphoṭa* is more and more definitely revealed till it is finally and completely manifested by the perception of the last letter; and *sphoṭa*, thus revealed, is expressive of the sense. Thus, we observe that the perception of different letters is not causally related to the cognition of sense; the perception of letters should rather be looked upon as being *anyathāsiddha* in so far as the cognition of sense is concerned.

CHAPTER TWO

1. *Kumārila on Sphoṭa*

THE GRAMMARIANS' THEORY MAKES NO IMPROVEMENT

The theory of *sphoṭa*, as we have explained in the previous chapter, has been strongly criticised by the Pūrvamīmāṁsakas. And, both the criticism and the rejoinder to the same by the grammarians go to testify to the sharp critical acumen of Indian philosophers. Kumārila opens his criticism of the theory of *sphoṭa* by asserting that the difficulties which confront us when we say that letters are expressive of sense, are sure to crop up with the grammarians' theory of *sphoṭa*. Do letters singly or conjointly reveal *sphoṭa* ? — asks Kumārila. And, he claims that the theory of *sphoṭa* is not immune from the charges that are levelled against the theory of the Mīmāṁsakas.[1]

Kumārila points out that letters cannot reveal *sphoṭa* singly for the obvious reason that if any one letter in a particular word is competent to reveal *sphoṭa,* the remaining letters will obviously be redundant. The grammarians meet the objection by saying that *sphoṭa* will be revealed on the very moment when the first letter is perceived; but, it becomes more and more definitely manifested with the perception of each one of the succeeding letters. Vācaspati, Maṇḍana and Jayanta elucidate the viewpoint of the grammarians by means of an illustration. A piece of diamond is recognised as such at the very first glance but the actual worth and excellence of the gem can exactly be determined only on careful observations for a number of times. That being so, later observations cannot be called futile; on the contrary, they are necessary for enabling us to determine precisely the worth of the gem. Thus, the first observation enables us to get a general or, rather, a rough knowledge of the object; while succeeding ones become necessary to know it more and more thoroughly till we arrive at a correct estimate.[2]

Hence, the grammarians maintain that with the perception of the first letter, *sphoṭa* is, no doubt, manifested; but, so long as the final letter is not perceived, it is not definitely and clearly revealed.[3] And, so, Kumārila's apprehension that succeeding letters will be redundant, is absolutely without any foundation.

It has been argued, however, that if letters in their respective capacities manifest *sphoṭa* more and more clearly, there is no reason whatsoever why they should not be expressive of sense in like manner. To be precise, the first letter will express the required sense in a more or less general way, while following letters will express the same more and more definitely till it is fully expressed with the perception of the final letter.

KUMĀRILA'S ANALOGY DOES NOT HOLD GOOD

But, we may be permitted to point out that the analogy does not unfortunately hold good. It is an established fact that we can speak of the imperfect or doubtful character of any perceptual knowledge, but never so of any non-perceptual knowledge.[4] In a case of any non-perceptual knowledge, our knowledge is sure to be definite and perfect in view of the fact that the causes in this case are required to be known. If the causes happen to remain unknown, we shall not be in a position to obtain the knowledge at all. Thus, we do or do not infer the existence of the fire on a hill-top from the sight of the smoke according as we have or have not beforehand the knowledge of the invariable concomitance of the probans with the probandum (i.e., of the smoke with the fire), of the probans itself and of the fact that the probans resides in the minor term. In the case of a perception, to the contrary, our knowledge is at times of an imperfect or doubtful character. For, when we see a person from a long distance we cannot exactly say whether he is sitting or standing, whether he comes this way or goes farther. It is only on closer observations that we are in a position to say what he is actually doing.

To come to the point, we have stated more than once that *sphoṭa* is cognised by mental perception; and, as in a perceptual knowledge, the object of cognition is said to be gradually revealed, it may be logically maintained that *sphoṭa* also is gradually manifested. But, we can by no means maintain that the import is more and more clearly expressed with the perception of each one of the succeeding letters for the obvious reason that the apprehension of the import is after all a piece of non-perceptual knowledge.[5]

Moreover, *sphoṭa* is never revealed in its entirety by anyone of the constituent letters. It is revealed only when all letters are successively pronounced. And, the meaning is expressed by *sphoṭa* when it is revealed in its entirety. The objection of partial expression of meaning, therefore, cannot arise as imperfect manifestation of *sphoṭa* is never assumed to be possessed of the expressive power.

ANOTHER ANSWER TO KUMĀRILA'S OBJECTIONS

We have so long discussed one of the modes of answer which the grammarians advance to the difficulties raised by Kumārila. But, we shall do well to note that Kumārila has also been answered in a different way. Thus, the grammarians opine that letters are nothing more than mere appearances and that *sphoṭa* is revealed by sound (*dhvani*) and not letters. Sound is said to be the breath-wind and as the breath-wind comes into contact with or strikes against different vocal organs, it apparently assumes different forms which we call letters.[6] Jayanta, while stating the grammarians' viewpoint, says that the breath-wind by reason of its unsteady character seems to represent vowel and consonant sounds which have no metaphysical existence. Now, it may be a fair question to ask that there being in reality no such entity as letter, how it is possible for the sound to represent it. The answer to this anomaly has been given by the grammarians in the following way. They point out that what is unreal may appear to be real through the medium of a distinguishing mark (*upādhi*).[7] A really lovely face reflected in a dirty mirror appears to be ugly; a round object reflected in a sword, a gem or a mirror, assumes different shapes. The sound produced by a lute, flute, drum or kettledrum seems to be different in nature.[8] Vācaspati asserts that the different attributes of letters [i.e., of their being short or long, acute (*udātta*), grave (*anudātta*) or circumflex (*svarita*), nasal or non-nasal] are imposed on them to serve practical purposes only. When we have, for instance, an '*a*' (short) attached to '*n*' as in '*nagaḥ*', we mean a mountain; but if it be an '*ā*' (long), the meaning changes and we understand an elephant.[9] Now, it is said that *sphoṭa* is revealed by the entire length of sound and not part by part. For instance, *sphoṭa* underlying a particular word is revealed when the whole word is uttered. It is not to be supposed that it is revealed letter by letter. So, the objection of Kumārila does not affect the doctrine of *sphoṭa* as the conditions of revelation of *sphoṭa* are entirely different from those imagined by Kumārila.

2. *Sabara on Sphoṭa*

ŚABARA SURVEYS THE WHOLE PROBLEM

We have fully discussed Kumārila's position and let us propose to enter into a critical examination of Śabara's observations on this subject. Śabara discusses the propriety of Upavarṣa's theory according to which word (*śabda*) means a number of letters and not *sphoṭa*.[10] Śabara apparently starts with a criticism of the theory of the great master; but, he intents to bring out the implicit meaning and excellence of the said theory. At the outset, Śabara maintains that word cannot imply letters for the obvious reason that if it does so, we shall not be able to explain how sense is expressed — is it expressed by letters singly or conjointly ? We have already discussed in a preceding chapter that either of the two alternatives is untenable. The first alternative cannot be accepted on the ground that the import is not obtained with the perception of any one of the letters. As for the other one, it may be said that letters being transient and not admitting of being pronounced simultaneously, cannot be said to form an aggregate. We have also seen that the supposition of individual recollections of the previously perceived letters at one and the same time enabling us to have the aggregate of letters required for, cannot be logically substantiated. Moreover, if individual letters are said to be recollected in succession, we can never get hold of an aggregate of letters; because, recollection, too, like perception, is transient and dies out on the third moment.[11]

Having raised these difficulties for himself, Śabara passes on to set forth his own conclusions. Thus, he opines that the continuous effects (*saṁskāra*)[12] accruing from the perception of successive letters up to the final one, will never die but the whole of the past *effects* running concurrently with the perception of successive letters will all live in the present perception of the final letter, together forming an aggregate giving expression to the idea of a word.[13] What Śabara states may be expressed in the following way. The Mīmāṁsakas posit a metaphysical link called *saṁskāra* or *apūrva* between a piece of work and its result. All actions bear fruits either good or bad. Now, there is in a majority of cases an interval between the performance of an act and the result that it bears. And, it cannot be maintained that an act performed this day is capable of effecting the result at a distant date. The Mīmāṁsakas, therefore, posit that before passing away, an act gives rise to some unknown effect (*adṛṣṭa*). Jaimini assumes the existence of an unseen force which may be regarded as the imperceptible antecedent of the fruit or as the after-state of an act. It has been stated in the Vedas that a man who wishes to go to heaven is required to perform a sacrifice. But, it is a well-known fact that the man does not repair to heaven as soon as he completes the prescribed sacrifice. Hence, the Mīmāṁsakas maintain that with the performance of a sacrifice, an unseen force is born and does not die out before it produces the effect. On this analogy, Śabara opines that the perception of each letter will give rise to an effect (*saṁskāra*) which will last even when the final letter is perceived; and, the final letter forming an aggregate with these individual effects will be expressive of sense.

ŚABARA'S EXPLANATION DOES NOT IMPROVE THE POSITION

But, such an explanation does not improve the position any further. For, the popular notion is that import is obtained directly from word (*śabda*) and not from the last letter forming an aggregate with the effects (*saṁskāra*) resulting from the perception of preceding letters. Moreover, such a procedure is not warranted by authoritative texts. Yāska himself says that a word ending in a verbal inflexion (*ākhyāta*), e.g. '*pacati*,' '*gacchati*,' etc. expresses an action (*bhāva*) that forms the meaning of the root.[14] Śabara boldly declares that he is not prepared to accept *sphoṭa* on the ground that popular notions cannot be justified. He makes no secret of the fact that popular notions are not always correct; and it will be unwise on our part to posit an unwarranted entity like *sphoṭa* for the simple reason that we cannot justify an incorrect popular notion. But, Śabara does not stop here. He goes a step further and openly declares that not only popular notions but even authoritative texts should not always be relied upon, if they fail to stand to reason.[15]

Śabara realises, in all probability, the far-reaching significance of his remark and, so, he turns round and explains his own point. He suggests that, as letters cannot form an aggregate by themselves, the last letter will form the same in conjunction with the effects (*saṁskāra*) which are but the after-state of the perception of preceding letters. But, he clearly points out that the causal relation between perception of letters and cognition of sense is not thereby destroyed. It may be legitimately argued that the causal relation, thus explained, becomes indirect. But, Śabara holds that in all cases of causal relation, the operation (*vyāpāra*) of the cause intervenes between the cause and the effect. To come to the point, some operation is necessary in order that the effect may be produced; and, as *saṁskāra* is regarded as an operation of the preceding letter for purposes of the expression of meaning, the causal relation may fairly be called direct.[16] Śabara, however, admits that he is even prepared to view this causal relation as indirect (*gauṇa*); but, he will never acknowledge an entity which is not cognised through any one of the cognitive instruments (*pramāṇa*).[17]

Śabara concludes his discussion on *sphoṭa* by asserting that the term 'word' means letters and not *sphoṭa*. He also shows that an aggregate of letters is possible. And, he finally asserts that the grammarians' theory is based on two unwarranted assumptions.[18] In the first place, the grammarians are required to posit *sphoṭa* itself; and secondly, they must admit that the impressions (*saṁskāra*) due to the perception of letters are competent to manifest *sphoṭa*.[19] But, the Mīmāṁsakas do not posit any such spiritual entity as *sphoṭa*. They only assume that *saṁskāras* are capable of expressing the required sense.

A MISCONCEPTION CLEARED UP

Before we proceed to criticise Śabara's theory, it needs to be mentioned that the grammarians always describe *sphoṭa* as an entity which is directly perceived; it is never posited (*kalpya*) by them to account for the cognition of sense. It may be pointed out in this connection that Jayanta while summing up the position that seeks to establish *sphoṭa*, says that *sphoṭa* may be cognised by inference (*anumāna*) or implication (*arthāpatti*); but, this observation of Jayanta should be interpreted in the light of a rejoinder given by the grammarians to the views of the Naiyāyikas.[20] For, as we have already observed, Jayanta himself has represented the grammarians' conception of *sphoṭa* by stating that *sphoṭa* is cognised through auditory perception.

CRITICISM OF ŚABARA

Let us now examine the merits or otherwise of Śabara's theory. The grammarians maintain that Śabara admits a number of unseen forces (*apūrva*) accruing from the perception of letters; yet, he is unwilling to admit that it is *sphoṭa* which is endowed with the power of expressing sense. Vācaspati humorously puts it that he fails to understand why Śabara is so very hostile to the grammarians that he is prepared to posit a number of unseen forces but declines to acknowledge *sphoṭa*.[21]

We, however, propose to criticise Śabara's theory from a different standpoint. According to Śabara, the final letter forming an aggregate with the perceptional effects (*saṁskāra*) is expressive of sense. Now, it is admitted on all hands that a perceptional effect is never perceived but is inferred from the result (*kāryānumānaikagamya*). That being so, it is not possible for us to know that the perception of each one of the letters gives birth to an effect (*saṁskāra*) unless sense is cognised. Hence, Śabara's statement involves the fallacy of interdependence. Again, we have said before that in the case of non-perceptual knowledge, the causes are required to be known prior to our obtaining the knowledge; and verbal knowledge being non-perceptual, it is only necessary that the knowledge of the final letter forming an aggregate with the effects (*saṁskāra*) should be present before we expect to obtain the cognition of sense. Now, the knowledge of the last letter forming an aggregate with the effects, being a qualified cognition (*viśiṣṭa-jñāna*), it is also necessary that we should be possessed of the knowledge of the effects (*saṁskāra*), i.e., the attribute (*viśeṣaṇa*) in this case, before we expect to obtain the knowledge of the last letter, that is, the substantive (*viśeṣya* or *dharmin*), forming an aggregate with the effects (*saṁskāra*).[22] Hence, to say that the final letter forming an aggregate with the effects (*saṁskāra*) resulting from the perception of preceding letters, causes the cognition of sense is logically unsound.[23]

3. *Jayantabhaṭṭa on Sphoṭa*

OBJECTION RAISED BY JAYANTA

We have discussed the views of Kumārila and Śabara on the theory of *sphoṭa*. And, now, it rests with us to examine the merits of the criticism put forth by Jayanta. We have stated before that *sphoṭa* is more and more clearly manifested with the perception of each one of the succeeding letters; and, we have cited the well-known illustration of a piece of gem in this connection. Jayanta, however, observes that the analogy does not hold good. Thus, he says that *sphoṭa* being an indivisible entity, it is hardly reasonable to opine that some of its parts will be manifested with the perception of the first letter, while others with that of the second and so on until all its parts are completely revealed with the perception of the final letter. In the case of a piece of gem, however, we are justified in maintaining that some of its parts are cognised at the first sight, others at a second glance and the rest gradually. There is every chance that some parts will escape our notice at the time of the first or the second observation and our knowledge of the object may be perfect at the fifth or the sixth time. But, it is certainly wrong to say that an object which does not admit of any division into parts will be gradually manifested.[24]

THE GRAMMARIANS' STANDPOINT FURTHER EXPLAINED

The objection of Jayanta seems to be unanswerable and, in fact, it has not been so much anticipated by Maṇḍana and other previous writers. But, we meet the difficulty exactly along the lines that have been followed by the Vedāntists. The *Brahman* is the only reality according to Vedānta and the *Brahman* which is absolute consciousness, is self-revealing and does not require the help of a medium to reveal itself. The medium, on the other hand, covers and veils its existence and the help of the cognitive instruments is required to remove this veil of matter or ignorance. Likewise, *Sphoṭa* is described as the *Śabda-brahman*, the Ultimate Reality and prius of the manifested world is absolutely destitute of all distinctions. The *Śabda-brahman* is the homogeneous, undivided, uniform existence and its apparent divisions are due to *avidyā*, which are rather superimposed on it. Bhartṛhari is never tired of emphasising the impartite differenceless character of the *Śabda-brahman*, which is the only reality behind this stupendous appearance, the magnificent show, the colossal hoax, which the phenomenal world is. The divisions, therefore, are absolutely illusory. But, though illusory, they are none the less felt by us who are in the grip of ignorance and, so, from the standpoint of the finite ignorant subject, the divisions, though they have no ultimate reality and are only false appearances, are believed to be real divisions. It does not, therefore, lie in us to question the empirical validity of these distinctions and, so, *Sphoṭa* has got to be revealed part by part as the medium of revelation is so constituted. The light of the sun covers the whole expanse of the world, it is only the barriers of the world that shut it off and divide it into compartments. *Sphoṭa* is self-revealing, but, that does not mean that it reveals itself to those who are separated by barriers from its light and illumination. The barriers may be the creation of our ignorance; but, they are there none the less and, as such, cannot be overcome except by the transcendental knowledge of the Ultimate Reality which is the highest consummation to be achieved, but not yet a realised experience with our finite intelligence. So, for our knowledge, *Sphoṭa* has of necessity to be revealed through vocal sounds just as the Absolute Spirit, the *Brahman* has got to be realised in and through the cognitive instruments, the windows of the psychophysical organism through which the light comes from the Absolute. *Sphoṭa* is to be realised by us through the medium of sounds which are successively and gradually revealed to us and, so, *Sphoṭa*, whose revelation is bound up with the revelation of sounds, is perforce revealed to us bit by bit, in small doses. The objection, therefore, raised by Jayanta[25] and later on by Appaya-dīkṣita in his super-commentary, the *Kalpataru-parimala*,[26] is only a specious difficulty. It seeks to confuse the metaphysical with the psychological issues. That *Sphoṭa* is divisionless is a metaphysical truth, which is logically established and never endorsed by experience. Our experience is, however, subject to the limitations imposed by *avidyā* and it is owing to these limitations that *Sphoṭa* is revealed to us only in small doses and never in its plenary form, in its real essence and magnitude. The difficulties of the psychical apparatus should not be transferred to the Ultimate Reality. The difficulty as pointed out in the objection, therefore, is only the result of confusion of metaphysical and psychical issues which should be carefully kept apart and is, therefore, more apparent than real.

To sum up, we may point out that *sphoṭa* is manifested with the perception of the first letter; but the perceptions of succeeding letters are not futile on that account. For, in the case of words beginning with the same letter, e.g., '*kara*' and '*kula*', it is the perception of the second letter and the following (e.g., '*a*', '*r*' and '*a*' in the case of '*kara*' while '*u*', '*l*' and '*a*' in the case of '*kula*') that enables us to know that the *sphoṭa* manifested by the first letter in the one is not the same *sphoṭa* manifested by the first letter in the other, though the first letter in either of the two words is the same. Thus, when we say that with the perception of the second and the following letters *sphoṭa* is more and more clearly manifested, we mean that the perception of the second and the following letters enable us to distinguish the *sphoṭa* manifested by the first letter in a particular word from the *sphoṭa* manifested by the first letter in another.[27]

MANIFESTATION OF SPHOṬA CLEARLY EXPLAINED

Let us speak a few more words on the manifestation of *sphoṭa* through the medium of letters. The letters in succession may be looked upon as a series which is the self-representation of *sphoṭa* itself. We have the characteristic of each member of the series in this that it represents the whole. The whole belongs to eternity, but yet posits itself in distinctions which are superseded in its comprehension of them. The whole is present in every part of it and every part of it implies the whole (*sphoṭa*).[28] The element of exclusion by which one phase is distinguished from another is a real phase, yet it is not all. It is a phase whose nature is to be forthwith put past and taken up into a higher comprehension. The part must be there as taken up and preserved in a more complete comphrehension. The endless aspect of the series is in contradiction with the fact of its limit and, therefore, a higher standpoint for the purpose of which the lower is inadequate but necessary for the solution of the contradiction and the comprehension of the whole, must be taken into consideration. *Sphoṭa* includes these distinct letters which go to make up the series to preserve them, not a mere series but in a higher conception in which they are comprehended in the eternity in which the series is summed up. Every letter is but an aspect in its own self. It comprehends its unity with the differences in this that the differences turn out to fall within itself and to form one whole with itself, the totality which embraces them.

We have here a succession of letters which is a great deal more than a succession of isolated units unconnected with one another. The meaning of each arises from its relation to the whole of the conception and the whole is present in every part of it. This is because each member of the series is something else than a mere isolated unit. The whole series may be viewed as given in its entirety in the whole (*sphoṭa*); and, consequently, as implicit in each member of the series. In the relation of each member to the others, we have got the law of the whole that enables us to sum it up; and in that way we have got the series in which it can be viewed as given in its entirety, in its law and implicitly given in its entirety in every member of the series. Thus, we are capable of comprehending the totality of the series for, in each stage, it comprehends the series as a whole. It is only on the basis of this eternity and within it that change has any meaning. Each phase alike, therefore, is what it is but also implicitly something other than what it is. It is, therefore, self-transcendent containing within itself necessary conditions of all else which is to be.

The parts are only the barriers through which the whole has got to reveal itself to finite minds. In its transcendental self-existence, the parts are simply *non est* and the whole reveals itself in its infinite simplicity. But, in the empirical plane, the Absolute is perforce manifested only in a piecemeal fashion and, thus, though we are never permitted to have a face to face acquaintance with the infinite truth, we are not, nevertheless, entirely divorced from it.[29] The whole is present as the whole in parts, only its manifestation is partial due to the distorting medium through which the infinite is perpetually presented to us.

REVIEW OF JAYANTA'S CRITICISM

Jayanta has further pointed out that the theory of the manifestation of *sphoṭa* through the medium of sounds is also untenable. For, he asserts that if sounds were capable of manifesting *sphoṭa*, there would have been no difficulty on our part to understand the import of a word even when it is uttered so quickly that its constituent letters are not distinctly heard.

We, however, do not appreciate this part of Jayanta's criticism. For, to suit our practical purposes alone, sounds have been divided into two categories, according to whether they do or do not manifest *sphoṭa* which is expressive of sense. To the yogin, however, each sound serves to manifest *sphoṭa* and he reads a meaning in every form of it. Thus, the moaning of the wind, the murmuring of the rivulet, the clattering of weapons, the pattering of rains, the roaring of the lion and the hissing of the snake, all have a meaning to the yogin who has concentrated his mind on word, sense and cognition and to whom the ultimate transcendental vision is perpetually a given fact.[30] But, to an ordinary man these sounds are entirely meaningless. Now, if an ordinary man says on that account that *sphoṭa* is not manifested by the murmur of the rivulet and that no meaning is expressed thereby, we can do nothing else but to request him to enter into the discipline of *śabda-tattva* as described in the Yoga system in Hindu philosophy. To come to the point, a word which is quickly uttered and the constituent letters of which are not clearly perceived, may not convey sense to those of us who are void of finer sensibilities; but, that does not mean that it is quite impossible to obtain the import in such a case. Individual incapacity to understand a thing cannot be held as an evidence for its non-existence.

As for Jayanta's insistence on the point that it is not proper to say that letters have no metaphysical existence of their own, our reply would be that the grammarians have taken recourse to various artifices to enable the beginner to gain an insight into the nature of *Śabda-tattva* and that they themselves declare that these artifices have no value of their own, they are but means to an end. It will be only transgressing the limits and encroaching on the exclusive province of the grammarians if we do not agree with them in determining the worth of these artifices which are but creations of their ingenious brain.

CHAPTER THREE

CLASSIFICATION OF SPHOṬA

1. INTRODUCTION

Nāgeśabhaṭṭa in his *Parama-laghu-mañjūṣā* enumerates no less than eight varieties of *sphoṭa* — *varṇa-sphoṭa, pada-sphoṭa, vākya-sphoṭa, varṇa-jāti-sphoṭa, pada-jāti-sphoṭa, vākya-jāti-sphoṭa, akhaṇḍa-pada-sphoṭa* and *akhaṇḍa-vākya-sphoṭa.*[1] It should be noted however, that of all these eightfold divisions it is *akhaṇḍa-vākya-sphoṭa* which alone represents *sphoṭa*, the other seven being creations of an ingenious brain for the purpose of enabling the student to comprehend the nature of the first. That these seven classifications have been mentioned and described with this end in view, is clearly discernible from Kṛṣṇa-bhaṭṭa's illumining observations on this point. Kṛṣṇa-bhaṭṭa says that though the seven divisions have no real value of their own, they still carry some practical utility. He points out that in the Advaita system of Vedānta philosophy, the Absolute Brahman has been, first of all, identified with the *annamaya-kośa* and then successively with the *prāṇamaya-kośa*, the *manomaya-kośa*, the *vijñānamaya-kośa* and the *ānandamaya-kośa*; but, on each occasion, it is pointed out precisely and in clear terms that the Absolute Brahman is something different from the one with which it is identified. We, thus, find that when the student fully grasps the concept of the *annamaya-kośa*, he is told that the Absolute Brahman is not the *annamaya-kośa* but something else. Then, when he acquaints himself with a thorough conception of the *prāṇamaya-kośa*, he is told again that the Absolute Brahman is not the same thing as the *prāṇamaya-kośa* and the process continues till the student is able to form a definite idea about the real nature of the Absolute Brahman.[2] We may also take up another illustration. The young bride who is to see the *arundhatī* (a star in the constellation of the pleiades), is asked to fix her gaze upon the bigger star *vaśiṣṭha* (another star in the same constellation) and after she has done so, she finds the smaller star *arundhatī* twinkling by its side. So, it is said that the identification of the five *kośas* with the Absolute Brahman and fixing one's gaze upon the *vaśiṣṭha* are but means to determine the real nature of the Absolute Brahman and the location of the *arundhatī* respectively. Similarly, it is maintained by the grammarians that the seven divisions of *sphoṭa*, mentioned above, enable the beginner to know the nature of the *akhaṇḍa-vākya-sphoṭa*. With this brief introduction, we proceed to discuss the nature of *varṇa-sphoṭa*.

2. VARṆA-SPHOṬA

At the outset, it is necessary to point out that by *varṇa-sphoṭa* it is not meant that each and every letter is regarded as *sphoṭa* but the letter or letters constituting either a stem or a suffix are regarded as such. The term *sphoṭa* is derived from the √*sphuṭ* and it is defined in two ways. In the first place, *sphoṭa* is defined as an entity which is manifested by letters. Secondly, it is an entity from which sense emanates.[3] According to the second definition we may state that when stems and suffixes are found to be expressive of sense, they should be regarded as denotative of sense or *sphoṭa*.

But, the problem that arises in this connection may be expressed in the following way. So far as the question of the stem is concerned, there is hardly any difficulty in calling it *sphoṭa*. But, there is a difference of opinion in the matter of the suffix as the latter means either the *sthānin* or the *ādeśa*.[4] The grammarians maintain that in such words as *pacati*, *rāmaḥ*, etc., the *ādeśas*, viz., '*ti*' and '*ḥ*', are expressive of sense and not the *sthānins*, viz., '*-la*' and '*-su*'. The Pāṇ Sū. III. iv. 77, is regarded as an *adhikāra* or governing[5] rule and '*-tip*', '*-tas*', '*-jhi*'. etc., are all *ādeśas* in the place of '*-la*.' And it is contended by the grammarians that the '*-su*' having changed into '*-ḥ*' (as the case of *rāma-su-rāmaḥ*), it is the latter which is to be regarded as denotative of the meaning.

The Naiyāyikas, on the other hand, strongly assert that it is the *sthānin* and not the *ādeśa* that is endowed with the power of denotation. They criticise the view of the grammarians by pointing out that it is certainly more reasonable and economical to hold that the *sthānin* is really expressive of sense on the ground that there is no limit to the number of *ādeśas* while the *sthānin* is more or less of a fixed character. Besides, in such cases where the suffix elides,[6] the difficulty arises on the ground that we have to admit that a thing which is in the nature of non-existence is possessed of the power of expressing sense. Moreover, the Naiyāyikas maintain that *ādeśas* are not of a fixed character, and, each being different from the other, it is not possible for us to determine their nature. But, if it be argued that the fact that they all agree in being '*-la*', enables us to get hold of a common attribute which will serve to determine their nature, the Naiyāyikas would opine that it is in that case reasonable to accept '*-la*' alone as expressive of sense. In addition to the arguments mentioned above, the Naiyāyikas point out that in such *sūtras* as Pān. Sū. III. iv. 69, the reference invariably is to the *sthānin* and not the *ādeśa* and, further, that no authoritative text can be cited to prove that the *ādeśa* is expressive of import.

The grammarians, however, make a most fitting reply to all the charges levelled against them by the Naiyāyikas. According to Patañjali, word is one which is endowed with power of denotation. It is, therefore, argued that a man who has even little knowledge of '*-la*', does yet understand the meaning of such expressions as *pacati*, *gacchati* and the like. Hence, what is actually used in language should be regarded as *vācaka* and not what is necessary only for grammatical operations. The Naiyāyikas, however, assert that it is through mistake that the *ādeśa* is regarded as the *vācaka*. But, the grammarians enquire about the cause or causes of this error. It is admitted on all hands that in all cases of error, the object must contradict our mistaken cognition of it. When we take a rope for a snake or a mother-o'-pearl for a piece of silver, our knowledge of the snake or the piece of silver is contradicted by the rope or the mother-o'-pearl. But, in the case of a valid knowledge, there is no scope for such a contradiction. To come to the point, we see nothing which may go to contradict our observation that it is the *ādeśa* which is really expressive of sense. As to the charge that *ādeśa* being numerous, it is not desirable to maintain that they are denotative of sense, it is replied that the *sthānins*, too, are none the less numerous. It is, therefore, that the grammarians do not see any justification as to why the *ādeśa* should not be regarded as the denoter. Then, again, there is hardly any truth in the statement that the *sthānin* is fixed while the *ādeśa* varies. Koṇḍa-bhaṭṭa comments that different grammarians have wilfully accepted different *sthānins*.[7] The serious objection to the Naiyāyika theory is that it involves unnecessary cumbrousness (*gaurava*). According to the Naiyāyikas, the *sthānin* by itself cannot be regarded as *vācaka*, for it is replaced by the *ādeśa* on each occasion and is not, therefore, present. Hence, the Naiyāyikas have got to admit that the *sthānin* recollected by the *ādeśa* expresses sense. And, this involves unnecessary cumbrousness. The Naiyāyikas, as we have already said, claim the credit of economy; but, the manner in which they expound their theory makes them liable to the same charge as they themselves level.[8] Koṇḍa-bhaṭṭa says further that of all those that determine the denotation of words, usage (*vyavahāra*) is deemed to be the most important (*śakti-grāhaka-śiromaṇi*). That being so, the *ādeśa* which is actually found to be used in the language, should in the fitness of things be possessed of power of denotation. The grammarians again, raise a very interesting point. They point out that the Naiyāyikas believe that it is the '*-la*' which is endowed with the power of denotation and so, they put the following question : had '*-la*' been really capable of expressing sense it would have been only natural to expect that even at the stage of grammatical operations (e.g., when we have the form *bhū-la*, the '*-la*' not yet replaced by any one of the *ādeśas*), there would have been no bar to the sense being expressed. But it is admitted on all hands that we do not understand the meaning at that stage. To obviate the difficulty the Naiyāyikas point out that the meaning cannot be expressed until we have some particular order of letters. In the circumstances, the grammarians aver that the position of the Naiyāyikas is somewhat curious; for, after positing that it is the '*-la*' which alone is expressive of sense, they are further required to admit that the particular order, must also be regarded as the cause of denotation. The grammarians on the contrary, argue to their advantage that it is the particular order of letters that is endowed with the power of expressing import. But, even then, the grammarians cannot cross the zone of controversy. The problem they are yet to solve may be stated in the following lines. From what has been already said, it is not clear that letters in some particular order (comprised of the stem and the suffix as used in the language) will be expressive of sense. On the contrary, it seems that the particular order of the letters is endowed with the power of denotation. Koṇḍa-bhaṭṭa does not answer the question. Harivallabha, however, takes note of the fact and sets forth a really cogent answer. He says that if the particular order of letters be regarded as expressive of sense, the determining factor of *vācakatva* (expressiveness of sense) will be so many letters; but, if the letters (building up the stem and the suffix) in some order be regarded as *vācaka*, it is one *ānupūrvī* (order of letters) that will determine *vācakatva*;[9] so, there is every justification for discarding the Naiyāyika theory which involves unnecessary cumbrousness. The grammarians further hold that the Naiyāyika theory is open to yet another inconsistency. The Naiyāyikas maintain that the *kṛt* suffixes express the sense of the nominative while *tiṅ* suffixes are expressive of *bhāvanā*.[10] But, this distinction cannot be logically maintained if '*-la*' alone be regarded as the denoter. On the other hand, granting that the *ādeśa* is expressive of sense, we can boldly assert that when the *ādeśa* is a *tiṅ*, it denotes *bhāvanā* and when it is a *kṛt*, it expresses the sense of the nominative. Thus, it appears that the grammarians' theory of *varṇa-sphoṭa* according to which the stem and the suffix (we mean, the *ādeśa* and not the *sthānin*) are denotative of sense.[11]

We have already stated that Indian grammarians started with the physical analysis of words and sentences and gradually proceeded to grasp the remotest form of speech which is known to be *sphoṭa* or *śabda-tattva*. And, it is a fact that in the case of all philosophical discussions, we start with the most concrete and arrive at the most abstract. The Absolute Brahman, for instance, is identified in the first place with the *annamayakośa* which forms the most concrete portion in human bodies;[12] next, it is identified with the less concrete, the *prāṇamayakośa* and so on. Similarly, in our study of *sphoṭa*, we discuss *varṇa-sphoṭa* in the beginning and next propose to examine the nature of *pada-sphoṭa*.

3. PADASPHOṬA

In our discussion of *varṇa-sphoṭa*, we have observed that letters in some particular order are expressive of sense. That being an established fact, we may be justified in positing that word which is generally viewed as a combination of letters, is also denotative of sense.[13] It is argued by the advocates of *pada-sphoṭa* that we do not actually remember the sense as each letter is perceived. On the contrary, we understand the sense of the word as a whole, the word *ghaṭa* (jar) in its entirety expresses the required sense and it is never a fact that each one of the four letters (*gh*, *a*, *ṭ*, *a*) constituting the said word is expressive of a fraction of the entire sense. Besides, a letter cannot be supposed to express a portion of the sense on the ground that the same, by reason of its being endowed with the power of denotation, will be regarded as a nominal stem *prātipadika*[13] and, as such, the '*n*' in *dhanam*, *vanam*, etc., will drop. (*Cp*. Pāṇ. Sū. VIII. ii. 7). In addition to the arguments advanced above, it is said that a letter can never be regarded as a denoter or *vācaka*; for, had the letter been possessed of denotative power, the letter '*a*' in *rāmaḥ* would have expressed its sense even if it were uttered a few minutes after the first three letters viz., *r*, *ā* and *m*, have been pronounced. Hence, we find that the question of sequence arises when we are asked to explain how sense is expressed. And, when letters in some sequence are said to constitute a word, it is reasonable to believe that the same is endowed with the power of expressing import. Having, thus, established *pada-sphoṭa*, the grammarians enter into a more technical study of the subject. According to the grammarians, word (*pada*) is one which ends in a nominal declension (*sup*) or a verbal inflexion (*tiṅ*).[14] In our discussion of *varṇa-sphoṭa*, we have pointed out that both the stem and the suffix are expressive of sense. But, if we carefully examine the above statement, certain difficulties are sure to crop up. In such forms as *ghaṭena* (the instrumental singular of *ghaṭa*) it is very difficult to say which portion of the term is the stem and which again is the suffix. An ordinary man who is acquainted with the meaning of the term very accurately, will not be in a position to distinguish the stem from the suffix, in this particular case. Even a man who has made an extensive study of Sanskrit grammar, will find some difficulty in ascertaining whether the '*-na*' or the '*-ina*' is the suffix in the form *ghaṭena*, unless he accurately remembers the views of Patañjali on this point. The *Mahābhāṣya* on Pāṇ. Sū. VII. i. 12 rejects the portion '*ināt*' from the *sūtra* and strongly asserts that the '*-na*' and '*-at*' are the respective *ādeśas* in places of '*-ṭā*' (instrumental singular) and '*-ṅas*' (ablative singular). In his commentary on Pāṇ. Sū. VII. ii. 101, Haradatta asserts that the forms *nirjarasina* and *nirijarasāt* are also available. And, in order to strengthen his position, he opines that as the word *nirjara* ends in '*a*', the suffixes '*-ṭā*' and '*-ṅas*' will change into '*-ina*' and '*-at*' and he supports his view with the help of the dictum — *vipratiṣedhe paraṁ kāryam* (Pāṇ. Sū. I. iv. 2).[15]

But, even then, he is to get rid of another difficulty. The injunction, *sannipātalakṣaṇavidhir animittaṁ tadvighātasya* (*Paribhāṣā* lxxxv. PSS),[16] does not sanction the substitution of *nirjaras* for *nirjara*. And, therefore, Haradatta assumes that the said injunction does not function here and the forms, *nirjarasina* and *nirjarasāt*, are available. Bhaṭṭoji-dīkṣita in his *Siddhānta-kaumudī* raises a note of objection against the aforesaid statement of Haradatta. He openly declares that not only the two forms mentioned above are wrong but the forms, *nirjarasaiḥ* and *nirjarasya* (in the instrumental plural and the genitive singular respectively), are also equally incorrect for the obvious reason that all of them are not sanctioned by Patañjali.[17] Patañjali has openly rejected the two *ādeśas* '*-ina*' and '*āt*' and has inserted '*-na*' and '*-at*' in their places. He has taken recourse to the principle of *yoga-vibhāga*[18] in Pāṇ. Sū. VII. iii. 105 and with its help has justified the '*e*' in *ghaṭena*. Thus, after a careful review of the position of the school of Patañjali, we are sure that it is the '*-na*' in *ghaṭena* that should be looked upon as the *ādeśa* in the place of '*-ṭā*'. That being so, the Naiyāyikas point out to their advantage that to a man well up in the Science of Grammar, there will be hardly any difficulty in recognising the stem and the suffix; and, hence, there is no justification for positing *pada-sphoṭa*. The grammarians, however, assert that the aforesaid distinction between the stem and the suffix cannot be recognised in those cases where the *ādeśa* replaces both the stem and the suffix. Thus, Pāṇ. Sū. VIII. i. 21 enjoins that in the accusative, dative and genitive plurals of *yuṣmad* and *asmad*, the substitutes *vas* and *nas* will replace both the stem and the suffix. In that case it is impossible to find out the parts that should be regarded as the stem and the suffix respectively. So, the grammarians carry out their point and *pada-sphoṭa* is established.

4. VĀKYA-SPHOṬA

We have discussed the nature of *pada-sphoṭa* so far; and, we propose to dwell upon *akhaṇḍa-pada-sphoṭa* along with *akhaṇḍa-vākyasphoṭa* later on. For the present, let us concentrate on *vākya-sphoṭa*. We have already pointed out that from the empirical standpoint, the sentence is the unit of thought and expression. And, as such, it is only natural that the sentence should be endowed with the power of denotation. According to the grammarians, a sentence is one in which we have at least one word ending with a *-sup* termination and another with a *-tiṅ*. It has been argued in the case of *pada-sphoṭa*, that as the distinction between the stem and the suffix cannot be understood in some places, it is desirable that besides *varṇa-sphoṭa*, we are required to admit *pada-sphoṭa* too. Arguing on the same line, the exponents of *vākya-sphoṭa* point out that it is difficult to distinguish between one term (*pada*) and another in certain cases of assimilation (*sandhi*).[19] For instance, Koṇḍa-bhaṭṭa points out that in the case of '*hare'va*', the two terms that have combined are not clearly discernible on the ground that the '*e*' which is the substitute for the '*e*', the final letter of '*hare*' and '*a*', the first letter of '*ava*', may be, in the opinion of the grammarians, looked upon as the last letter of '*hare*' or the first letter of '*ava*'.[20] Hence, Koṇḍa-bhaṭṭa asserts that we should do well to recognise another type of *sphoṭa*.[21]

But, there is yet stronger justification for admitting *vākya-sphoṭa*. It cannot be denied that for purposes of communication of ideas, the sentence serves our purpose well. The child who is yet ignorant of the technicalities and principles of grammar understands the import of a sentence when between two persons, in its presence, it observes one to perform a certain act, after he has been told by another person to do the same. For instance, the child knows the meaning of the sentence 'Bring a cow' (*gām ānaya*), when it sees that the man to whom it is said, goes away and brings the animal. But, as it can hardly be said that the child knows the individual imports of the constituent words of the sentence, it is to be admitted that the sentence as a whole is endowed with the power of expressing sense; and, as such, *vākya-sphoṭa* is established. Koṇḍa-bhaṭṭa explicitly states that as words are capable of expressing meaning, so, sentences are possessed of the power of denotation. And, he establishes his point by maintaining that it is from such expressions as '*ghaṭam ānaya*' (bring a jar) that we understand some meaning but not from '*ghaṭaḥ karmatvam ānayanaṁ kṛtir iṣṭasādhanam*,' on the ground that in the latter case we have no sentence. And, if as the Naiyāyikas aver that for purposes of expressing sense expectancy (*ākāṅkṣā*) is necessary, the grammarians would like to suggest that this *ākāṅkṣā-śakti* is nothing different from the *vākya-śakti* as maintained by them. Jagadīśa in his *Śabda-śakti-prakāśikā* says it in so many words that *ākāṅkṣā* is reducible to *ānupūrvī*[22] which is defined as the sequence of letters. And, as letters in some particular sequence make up a sentence, there is hardly any inconsistency in the statement of Koṇḍa-bhaṭṭa when he emphatically says that the *ākāṅkṣā-śakti* of the Naiyāyikas is identical with the *vākya-śakti* of the grammarians.[23] Thus, we notice how Koṇḍa-bhaṭṭa seeks to establish *vākya-sphoṭa.*

Now, the Naiyāyikas point out that the cognition of the import of a sentence, being in its nature a qualified knowledge,[24] cannot be obtained prior to the verbal knowledge (*śābda-bodha*)[25]; and, as such, it is not possible for us to know how the sentence by itself is endowed with the power of expressing sense. But, the import of a term may be known prior to the verbal knowledge. Hence, it is argued that it is the term which is possessed of the power of expressing sense. But, the grammarians take up the challenge and solve the difficulty in an efficient manner. It is held that the Prābhākaras opine that the import of a term includes 'relation' (*anvaya*) in its general character; but, it is only when the verbal knowledge is obtained that we come to know of this relation in its special bearings.

PRĀBHĀKARA THEORY OF VERBAL KNOWLEDGE

According to the Prābhākaras, the meaning of a term implies not merely what the Bhāṭṭas and the Naiyāyikas believe it to be, but something in addition. The denoted sense implies the import of the individual term qualified by the relation that subsists between it and the senses of other terms in the sentence under consideration to which it is related. The Prābhākaras maintain that in our everyday use, we communicate our ideas by means of sentences and not terms. So, it is natural that each term is required to be studied in relation to another and not separately by itself. Hence, it is held that the import of a term cannot be identical with what the rival schools of philosophers believe it to be. Moreover, it is opined that relation must be shown as lying inherent in the import of the term on the ground that what does not present itself through the medium of terms cannot be the content of the verbal knowledge. But, it may be pointed out that this relation is expressed by the terms in a more or less general manner and it is only at the time of the verbal knowledge that this relation is precisely determined. For instance, in such expressions as 'Bring a jar' (*ghaṭam ānaya*), so long as we have not used the term '*ānaya*', the denoted sense of the term '*ghaṭam*' is the import of the term qualified by the relation that subsists between it and the import of another term; that is, the relation is not specifically ascertained. It is at the time of the verbal knowledge alone that we come to know of the same most accurately. Hence, the grammarians opine that the import of a sentence is known to us in a general way before the verbal knowledge of the same is obtained; and, it is the peculiar character of a sentence that enables us to cognise it accurately at the time of the verbal knowledge.

FURTHER POINTS IN SUPPORT OF VĀKYA-SPHOṬA

We have so long been occupied with the discussion of a very knotty point to show that sentences are really possessed of the power of expressing sense. But, we may point out that there are reasons more simple yet none the less convincing for the acceptance of *vākya-sphoṭa*.

It has been maintained that in the case of such sentences as 'There is a hamlet of cowherds on the deep river' (*gabhīrāyāṁ nadyāṁ ghoṣaḥ*), we cannot get at the meaning unless we believe that it is the sentence which is endowed with the power of expressing import. The Naiyāyikas argue that the term '*nadyām*' means the river-side through its power of implication (*lakṣaṇā*). But, the difficulty crops up when we ask them to construe the import of the term '*gabhīrāyām*' with it. It is admitted on all hands that in the case of apposition (*sāmānādhikaraṇya*)[26] specially, the import of one term cannot be construed with a part of the import of another term. In the present case, the import of the term '*gabhīrāyām*' is related to that of '*nadyām*'; but, if we, through the help of implication, understand the river-side by the term '*nadyām*', the import of the term '*gabhīrāyām*' cannot be construed with it. The Naiyāyikas have seen through the difficulty; but, the solution they suggest is far from being satisfactory. They say that the term '*nadyām*' means the side of a deep river (*nadyām=gabhīranadītīre*). But, in that case, the term '*gabhīrāyām*' becomes redundant. The Naiyāyikas still argue that the aforesaid term is necessary in view of the fact that it helps us to understand the nature of the meaning which the term '*nadyām*' expresses through its power of implication. This argument carries little weight, for, in all cases of implication, such terms are not available enabling us to ascertain the nature of the implied sense.

COMPOUND WORDS ARE POSSESSED OF A SPECIAL POWER

From what has been discussed above, it becomes clear that it is necessary to accept *vākya-śakti*. It will be our endeavour now to point out that in the case of compounded words which are regarded as *mahā-vākyas* by the Naiyāyikas, it becomes absolutely indispensable to accept a *śakti* of compounds to express the required sense. Thus, the grammarians point out that in the case of possessive compounds (*bahuvrīhi*), a difficulty arises in the matter of construing the senses of the members of the compound. For instance, the word '*ambara*' in the compound '*pītāmbara*' does not mean 'garment' but 'the person who wears the garment' (*ambara-viśiṣṭa*). Hence, the import of '*pīta*' cannot be logically construed with the import of '*ambara*', for reasons mentioned in a preceding paragraph.[27] It is why the grammarians acknowledge a special *śakti* of compounds; and this *śakti* is technically called *ekārthībhāva*.[28] Thus, the grammarians point out that a compound never expresses the senses of its components merely, but always conveys one united sense based on the meanings of its members. Hence, in the case of *rājñaḥ puruṣaḥ*, we may add as many epithets to *rājñaḥ* as we like; but, in the case of the compound '*rājapuruṣaḥ*', we cannot qualify it in like manner. The Naiyāyikas, however, do not admit the aforesaid *śakti* of compounds for the only reason that it is unnecessary. But, the grammarians assert that there are a good many cases where the sense of the compound differs perceptibly from the combined senses of the components. Moreover, they argue that the Naiyāyikas are required to frame many rules for the purpose of explaining many critical points on this subject.[29] Thus, we may conclude that when the compound which is regarded as a sentence (*samasta-vākya*) after all, is endowed with the power of expressing sense, it is certainly reasonable to hold that sentences are also expressive of sense. And, so, *vākya-sphoṭa* is established.

SENTENCES ARE ENDOWED WITH THE POWER OF IMPLICATION (LAKṢAṆĀ)

We may further argue in our favour that the Mīmāṁsakas have recognised the power of implication in the case of sentences. Students of the Pūrva-mīmāṁsā system of philosophy know it thoroughly well that the *arthavāda-vākyas*[30] do not embody positive injunctions but are meant to eulogise Vedic injunctions.[31] They carry no meaning in themselves but let us know that Vedic injunctions are efficacious. Hence, the Mīmāṁsakas maintain that each sentence which contains an *arthavāda* refers to the excellence of the injunction through its power of implication. Such being the case, one may argue that the sentence which is not possessed of the power of denotation as the Mīmāṁsakas maintain, should not be supposed to be endowed with the power of implication.

We have fully discussed the problem whether the sentence by itself is expressive of sense and have stated precisely and in clear terms that the sentence is endowed with the power of denotation. And, we close this section by pointing out once more that the history of languages reveals this fact that as the sentence is the unit of thought and expression, it will be the height of folly to disown its denotative power.

5. JĀTI-SPHOṬA

We have so far discussed the nature of *varṇa-sphoṭa*, *pada-sphoṭa* and *vākya-sphoṭa* and now propose to enter upon a study of another three varieties : *varṇa-jāti-sphoṭa*, *pada-jāti-sphoṭa* and *vākya-jāti-sphoṭa*. Both Bhaṭṭoji-dīkṣita and Koṇḍa-bhaṭṭa say that according to Bopadeva, the denoter or *vācaka* like the denoted or *vācya* should be of the nature of the universal (*jāti*). The Mīmāṁsakas have discussed the question of the import of words and they maintain that the individual (*vyakti*) cannot be regarded as the import for the reason that there is no limit to the number of individuals and that they vary widely amongst themselves. It is, therefore, that they have sought to find out one common attribute (*sādhāraṇa-dharma*), technically known as the universal (*jāti*) which is present in each one of the individuals within the universal; and this universal is denoted by a word. The exponents of *jāti-sphoṭa* argue that when the import that is denoted is the universal, it is reasonable to admit that what expresses sense is also of the nature of the universal. Hence, it is not that the individual word '*hari*' uttered by a certain person is expressive of sense but the universal which finds its expression through the different use of the said word, is significant.[32] And, this is the conception of *pada-jāti-sphoṭa*. Similarly, we have *varṇa-jāti-sphoṭa* and *vākya-jāti-sphoṭa*.

Before we close this section, we would like to point out that the exponents of *jāti-sphoṭa* in their endeavour to assert that it is *jāti-sphoṭa* and not *vyakti-sphoṭa* which is expressive of sense, have in their mind the conception of *Mahājāti* (*Mahāsāmānya* or *Mahāsattā*) or *Brahman* with which *Sphoṭa* has been identified.

6. AKHAṆḌA-SPHOṬA

We have discussed the nature of *jāti-sphoṭa* and its threefold divisions. Next, we propose to explain *akhaṇḍa-pada-sphoṭa* and *akhaṇḍa-vākya-sphoṭa*. The grammarians assert that neither the sentence nor the word admits of any divisions. It has been definitely stated that letters have no metaphysical existence. Bhartṛhari openly declares that word does not comprise letters.[33] On more occasions than one it is said that the division of word into stems and suffixes has been resorted to for practical purposes alone.[34] The devices employed in standard works in course of treatment of linguistic problems are at best of a pragmatic value. It will be a grievous error of judgment to suppose that these divisions are ultimately true. They are only ways and means devised to inculcate the final truth, and, in and by themselves, they are not possessed of any metaphysical value. But, though figments of imagination, they are not useless as they definitely contribute to the comprehension of the truth. Even a staunch realist will admit that the means is of a lower status than the end, and all the value that the former possesses is derived from its capacity to contribute to the achievement of the end. The Vedāntists and the Mādhyamikas, too, recognise the serviceability of false standards of judgment.[35] So far as the Vedāntists and the grammarians are concerned, the pragmatic utility of fictitious standards can be logically proved from the fact that erroneous conceptions are ultimately grounded in truth inasmuch as they appear over the basic foundation of reality. Thus, the exponents of *akhaṇḍa-pada-sphoṭa* maintain that it is the indivisible word that is expressive of sense. But, it should be noted that the sentence being the unit of thought and expression should be endowed with the power of denotation and the exponents of *akhaṇḍa-vākya-sphoṭa* believe that it is the indivisible sentence which is expressive of sense. And, according to them, therefore, words, stems, suffixes and letters are absolutely fictitious.[36]

We have explained the eightfold division of *sphoṭa* as it has been treated in later standard works of Sanskrit grammarians; but, we should like to point out that we do not appreciate their conception of *pada-sphoṭa* and *vākya-sphoṭa* as also of *akhaṇḍa-pada-sphoṭa* and *akhaṇḍa-vākya-sphoṭa*. The difference between *pada-sphoṭa* and *akhaṇḍa-pada-sphoṭa* and that between *vākya-sphoṭa* and *akhaṇḍa-vākya-sphoṭa* has been stated by Kṛṣṇa-bhaṭṭa in his *Sphoṭa-candrikā*. He says that the difference between *pada-sphoṭa* and *akhaṇḍa-pada-sphoṭa* lies in the fact that in the case of *pada-sphoṭa*, there is a reference to the stem and the suffix which, however, have been so intermingled that it is difficult, if not totally impossible, to differentiate the one from the other and word is, therefore, conceived as being endowed with the power of denotation. In the case of *akhaṇḍa-pada-sphoṭa*, however, there is absolutely no reference to the stem and the suffix, rather, they are regarded as being fictitious and word as an indivisible unit expresses sense. Similarly, in the case of *vākya-sphoṭa*, it is the sentences which are said to be expressive of sense; but, these sentences are not conceived in their indivisible character — they comprise words and the constituent words are not clearly distinguishable. But, when we say that the indivisible sentence is expressive of sense, we think of *akhaṇḍa-vākya-sphoṭa*.[37]

NEW INTERPRETATIONS PROPOSED

We are prepared to accept such an interpretation; but, may we be permitted to say that such an interpretation serves only to diminish the glory and importance of the indivisible and transcendental character of *sphoṭa*. And, any interpretation which tends to impair the indivisible character of *sphoṭa*, cannot be accepted by us. It may be pointed out in our favour that the earlier exponents of the theory of *sphoṭa* mean by *pada-sphoṭa* and *vākya-sphoṭa* what to the later exponents are *akhaṇḍa-pada-sphoṭa* and *akhaṇḍa-*

vākya-sphoṭa respectively. Even Koṇḍa-bhaṭṭa in course of establishing *vākya-sphoṭa* argues that to a child who is yet ignorant of the conventions and technicalities of grammar, the sentences, certainly, indivisible into parts, are expressive of sense. Thus, we find that the aforesaid argument advanced apparently in support of *vākya-sphoṭa* by Koṇḍa-bhaṭṭa is in reality one in support of *akhaṇḍa-vākya-sphoṭa*.

Therefore, if we are to admit the two classifications, *akhaṇḍa-pada-sphoṭa* and *akhaṇḍa-vākya-sphoṭa*, we venture to interpret them as follows: By *akhaṇḍa-pada-sphoṭa*, we mean that there is one indivisible word which undergoes various formal transformations and this one indivisible word is expressive of sense. Likewise, we mean by *akhaṇḍa-vākya-sphoṭa* that there is one indivisible sentence which assumes a plurality of forms by undergoing formal transformations and this one indivisible sentence expresses import. The conception of *pada-sphoṭa* is that there are countless indivisible words, each expressing a particular meaning while the conception of *vākya-sphoṭa* is that there are numerous indivisible sentences each of which is possessed of the power of denotation.

CHAPTER FOUR

AUTHORITY OF ĀGAMA ON SPHOṬA

1. INTRODUCTION

We have endeavoured in the preceding pages to observe that Bhartṛhari has demonstrated with abundant logic that the identity of *Sphoṭa* is proved not only on the authority of perception but also of inference. And, it may be mentioned in this context that there is the sanction of *āgama* for its acceptance as well. So, we turn to the Āgama texts where *śabda* or word is described not merely as an aggregate of sounds but recognized as an indivisible identity.

According to Patañjali, author of the Yoga Sūtras, *pratyakṣa, anumāna* and *āgama* are the three *pramāṇas*.[1] *Āgama* is defined by Vyāsa as the knowledge of the hearer (*śrotṛ*) coming in the wake of hearing a verbal expression falling from the lips of the speaker (*vaktṛ*) who is an *āpta*.[2] An *āpta* person is described as one blessed with the vision of the truth, compassionate and possessing efficient senses.[3] Such a speaker transmits his own knowledge of objects obtained from perception or inference through the medium of words.[4] When such words are heard, the hearer acquires the knowledge of objects intended to be communicated by the speaker. The two knowledges, of the speaker and of the hearer, are not identical but similar to each other.[5] The knowledge of the hearer based on the words of the speaker is, in the language of Patañjali, a case of *āgama*.

Bhartṛhari also seems to accept the authority of all the three proofs of knowledge mentioned above viz., perception, inference and *āgama*. He is aware that neither the Cārvākas nor the Buddhists accept *āgama* as a *pramāṇa*. In his zeal to establish the authority of *āgama* as a *pramāṇa*, he mentions in an unambiguous tone not only the justification for its acceptance but he hastens to point out the incompetency of both perception and inference to help us in obtaining correct results in certain cases. *Āgama*, in the philosophy of Bhartṛhari, means both *Śruti* and *Smṛti*.[6] The Vedas have been described as the very image of the Eternal Verbum and the instrument for its realization. Though the Veda is one, yet there are four principal divisions of the same, each in its turn comprising a number of branches known as *śākhā*.[7] But, it is to be remembered that each branch of the Veda aims at the production of one particular result, viz., *apūrva* and that there is some fixed rule for determining the meaning of the text. It is said that the division into branches takes place from time to time. The idea is that the one Veda becomes divided due to the limitations of those who read it; in course of time, again, the divisions are withdrawn and it becomes one; after a lapse of time it becomes divided once again. This is why it is called *āgama*.[8]

Smṛti which is also called *āgama* has been formulated by those versed in the Vedas out of indications (*liṅga*) found in the Vedas. Grammar is held to be a *smṛti* work,[9] which is called the most important of all the six auxiliary sciences (*aṅga*) of the Vedas. This work being an *āgama*[10] was lost sometime only to be restored later on. The tradition of unbroken continuity is thus maintained. Bhartṛhari gives a vivid picture of how the Vyākaraṇa was lost when the work of Patañjali came to be misinterpreted and how Vasurāta, his teacher, could restore it to its former stature.[11] This *āgama* discusses the formation of chaste words as distinguished from *apabhraṁśas*. It may be mentioned that both chaste words and *apabhraṁśas* are equally expressive of sense but the former have been declared by the *śiṣṭas* to be the means for the attainment of religious merit.[12] It cannot be argued that the aforesaid declaration by the *śiṣṭas* is not convincing, because they are not found to make any futile statements. Chaste forms are as much significant as unchaste forms. So, it is held that use of chaste words begets religious merit. Like all other *smṛtis*, this *smṛti* also is *dṛṣṭādṛṣṭa-prayojana*; to be precise, it enables us to understand the meaning of words as also to acquire merit from the use of chaste forms. It has to be admitted that it has a claim to be reckoned as a *pramāṇa*. For, it is not for perception or inference to inform us about what is *dharma* or *adharma*.[13] Āgama, Veda and Smrti, like perception and inference, is, therefore, a *pramāṇa*, an instrument of valid knowledge, nay, the most competent one.

In his zeal to advocate the authority of *āgama*, Bhartṛhari has made some important observations which seem to have been misunderstood and misinterpreted. Let us pursue the points in detail. In the first place, it is held that there are seers who, with the help of the 'third eye' can visualize things which ordinary mortals fail to see. It is indeed very difficult to divine how they obtain the excelling knowledge of seeing the past and the future, the subtle and the distant. The answer is that it is because of their rigid and careful adherence to the injunctions of *āgama* that they obtain the specific efficiency enabling them to perceive things that lie beyond the ken of ordinary perception.[14] It is not possible to perceive how the meanings expressed by chaste words are competent to bring about success in life, (*abhyudaya*); and it also does not lie with inference to tell us that the effects would be produced not at the time the words are spoken and heard but in some distant future. Bhartṛhari points out in emphatic terms that the seers on whom the Light has descended and who are purged of ignorance can know objects belonging to the past and the future with such vividity that it is as much informative as ordinary perception. And, as such, we should not question the authority of such knowledge with the employment of inference. Bhavabhūti, the poet, asserts that the words of those who have been blessed with spiritual vision are not tainted by doubt for what they say is never false.[15] It is mentioned that seers who have themselves visualised the Truth see the Supersubtle Eternal, the Supersensuous Word and feel the urge to communicate it to others who have not as yet been fortunate to realize it; and, for this purpose they seek the aid of a symbol, i.e. the Veda and its auxiliaries just in the same way as one relates one's dream-experience, what he has seen, heard and experienced, on the termination of his sleep. It becomes, therefore, crystal clear that the Veda is the truth par excellence. And, even though there have been times when Veda and Smṛti fell into a desuetude, yet, there is an unbroken tradition among *śiṣṭas* who have taken special care to maintain its continuity. Bhartṛhari is very eloquent when he, therefore, adumbrates the authority of *āgama* when he asks us not to dispute its validity with the help of inference. After all, *āgama* records the line-honoured paths of *dharma* which are universally accepted.

As it has been mentioned before, Bhartṛhari does not feel very happy about the competence of inference to acquaint us with the truth in all cases. He enumerates a few difficulties which stand in the way of drawing correct conclusions with the help of inference. The powers of the same object are found to vary in different circumstances, at different places and at different times: to be precise, it seems as though the nature of a thing changes, a fact that may create difficulties in deducing logical conclusions. The same kind of seeds or plants grown on a different soil have different properties. Water is ordinarily cool to touch but the water of a hot spring[16] may be quite different. Further, objects possessed of definite causal efficiency are found to be inoperative in regard to other substances. Thus, for instance, fire possesses burning capacity which becomes inoperative on mica.[17] It is further stated that the results of an inference carefully drawn by a person may be changed by another gifted with a sharper intellect. He, further, states that if a blind person runs on a rough road by groping with his hand it is not unlikely that he will come to grief with a fall; so, a man who more often than not trusts his power of reasoning and does not depend in the least on *āgama* will be landed in sin.[18]

When Bhartṛhari mentions all these drawbacks of reasoning, it must be said that his intention is not so much to undermine the importance of inference or reasoning as a *pramāṇa* as to glorify the advantages of *āgama*. Āgama, comprising Śruti and Smṛti, enjoys an important stature as it helps us in the realization of the Ultimate Reality and the attainment of *abhyudaya* through the use of chaste forms of words coming in the wake of our acquaintance with grammar.

Bhartṛhari, while admitting perception as one of the *pramāṇas*, has warned us also against putting too much reliance on its efficiency in ascertaining the truth. Thus, he says that the vision of sages which is not different from perception[19] is correct indeed but it must not be forgotten that this is something transcendental. And, as we know that our empirical and intersocial communications cannot be conducted with transcendental experiences, it may be enquired how far our perceptual knowledge can be trusted in understanding the intersocial communications of our every-day life. To be precise, let perception decide what should be the meaning of words. But, is it not a fact that we all perceive the sky as a blue canopy and the fire-fly as a spark of fire? It is, therefore, in the fitness of things that Bhartṛhari points out the justification for testing our perceptual experiences with the help of reasoning. But, as it has been mentioned before, reasoning also sometimes fails to deliver the goods. Further, it is a matter of common knowledge that visual perception is not competent to enable us in obtaining knowledge of all the different parts of an object at one time — it is only possible to have the knowledge of a few parts and the rest may be inferrable for the time being.

It should not be presumed, that the grammarian-philosopher hesitates to accept the authority of inference or is critical about it.[20] For, reasoning, as Bhartṛhari avers, is a necessary aid for those who are not endowed with the penetrative eye to understand the meaning of the Veda. The laws (*nyāya*) of reasoning employed in the system of Mīmāṁsā have been formulated to that end.[21] It needs to be mentioned, however, that reasoning which goes against the very spirit of the Veda should not be encouraged. Reasoning must be compatible with the spirit of the Veda. It must be borne in mind that it is not possible to draw out the meaning of the Scriptures from their form only — the meaning has to be discovered with the help of reasoning.[22] It is for reasoning to arrive at the principles to be utilized for the purpose of determining the intended implications. It is also very interesting to notice that Bhartṛhari throws some light on what he understands by reasoning. It has to be admitted that reasoning rests in human intelligence; but, in the ultimate analysis it would appear that the same is the power of our verbal expressions. Speakers who are aware of this power select suitable expressions to convey the intended meaning. They are not found to select such expressions as are not competent to convey the same. Now, when the hearer tries to grasp that power of the word with the application of the principles of reasoning as laid down in authoritative texts, that reasoning is described as one which is located in the hearer. To be precise, reasoning that does not take into consideration the power of word may be deemed to be reasoning unproductive (*śuṣka-tarka*).[23]

2. SOME ŚRUTI TEXTS ON SPHOṬA

We have stated the theory of *sphoṭa* as adequately as possible. It will be our next endeavour to show from Vedic hymns and Brāhmaṇa texts that *śabda* is not merely an aggregate of letters and that it should be regarded as an indivisible entity having a transcendental character. ṚV. X. 71. 4. has found a brilliant and enlightening interpretation from the pen of Bharatamiśra who in his *Sphoṭa-siddhi* says that *śabda-tattva* unfolds itself in its naked glory to the man who has made both intensive and extensive study of the Science of Grammar and has been able to shake off his ignorance by meditating on word, sense and cognition. Such a man alone realizes that what we call mountains and rivers is nothing but the formal transformation of *śabda-tattva*. It is he who understands that, from the metaphysical point of view, letters do not constitute word or sentence.[24] Thereafter, Bharata-miśra takes up a Brāhmaṇa text — *saitaṁ mantram apaśyat*, and proves that therein we may find out a reference to *śabda-tattva*. He explicitly states that the expression — He (the sage) saw this hymn — means that the sage heard the hymn. But, as there must be a difference in the hearing of a hymn on our part and on that of the sage, it is implied that the sage who is gifted with high spiritual powers, hears the hymn at a stage when it is not uttered. And, the existence of a hymn at a time when it is not uttered, leads us to think that the hymn has a transcendental form, it is not merely the aggregate of a few letters as are ordinarily perceived through the auditory organ. The author of the *Sphoṭa-siddhi-nyāya-vicāra* has followed in the footprints of Bharata-miśra when he in some verses[25] of rare beauty has given expression to all that Bharata-miśra says on this point. Maṇḍana in his *Sphoṭa-siddhi* says that he has established the theory of *sphoṭa* on the authority of Āgama texts and the *Gopālikā* points out that Ṛv. X. 71. 4. is one of the Vedic hymns which testifies to the existence of *sphoṭa*.[26]

3. ŚABDA-YOGA

In the course of our thesis, we have sought to establish the theory of *sphoṭa* strictly in conformity with the great teachers of the past. We have, however, differed in certain points from the orthodox interpretations and we invite the critical acumen of the present-day scholars to judge the merits of our exposition. We have made a comprehensive survey of all the criticisms to which the theory of *sphoṭa* has been subjected and it has been our endeavour to solve each one of the difficulties raised. It should be borne in mind that all the orthodox systems of Hindu Philosophy, the Pūrva-mīmāṁsā, the Nyāya, the Vedānta and the Sāṅkhya[27] have spared no pains in criticising the theory and finally rejecting it. It is only the Yoga system of Patañjali which has lent support to the grammarian's theory of *sphoṭa*. Dr. Chakravarti takes note of this fact when he says: 'The theory of *Sphoṭa* seems to have a strange fate, as it failed to find any favourable response at the hands of reputed philosophers.'[28] But, we do not stop with him when he says : In spite of all adverse criticisms that have been heaped upon the assumption of an intellectual phenomenon as *Sphoṭa*, the theory of *Sphoṭa* will continue to survive as embodying the most reasonable and scientific interpretation about the origin of sound.[29] We proceed further to assert that *sphoṭa* is not merely the outcome of careful investigations in the domain of grammatical science, but the conception of *sphoṭa* embodies in itself a truth which speaks for itself. Thus, the grammarians have laid down a course of *sādhanā* of *sphoṭa* which, they believe, will lead the *sādhaka* on to emancipation to realise the true nature of Word-essence which is equated with the Absolute Brahman of the Vedānta — the *prius* of the entire phenomenal world, subjective and objective. There is absolutely no note of hesitancy, no faltering or apologetic tone in the representation of the grammarian-philosopher. On the contrary, we notice in it the same bold and emphatic deliverance of a direct realisation of the Truth as is found in the inspired utterances of the Mystics of the world. The impression insensibly and irresistibly is infiltrated into the deepest recesses of our heart that we are brought face to face with the Ultimate Mystery of the universe. Intellectual speculations in India were never content to find only an intellectual solution of the problems of life and the Truth discovered was rigorously pursued in and through a well-graduated scale of discipline until a direct and immediate realisation was reached. Of course, philosophy knew its limitations and left the scene as soon as it culminated in a rationalisation of experience. But, the goal of philosophy in India was not mere rationalisation but rather spiritualisation. Philosophy found its consummation in an enriched life, in the fulness of spiritual outlook, the highest perfection that ethical and intellectual discipline could aspire after. It always aimed at the inwardisation of the truth discovered and no philosophy which failed to end in this glorious expansion of spiritual life was deemed to be worthy of human allegiance. The Philosophy of Grammar also did not fail to emphasise this Ultimate Objective of life and like other philosophies ends in Mysticism (*sādhanā*).

The grammarian-philosopher describes grammar as the doorway to emancipation and declares with all emphasis and in the most unambiguous language that the ultimate purpose of the study of grammar is to secure emancipation (*apavarga*) which may be reached through communion known as *śabda-yoga* or *śabda-pūrva-yoga* or *vāg-yoga*. According to Bhartṛhari, the Ultimate Reality is the Eternal Verbum which is out-and-out a unitary principle (*ekam eva yad āmnātam*), a partless (*akhaṇḍa*) and sequenceless (*akrama*) identity which is manifested (*abhivyakta*) by sounds (*dhvani*) or syllables (*varṇa*) pronounced one after another in quick succession. It is the succession of sounds that is reflected, as it were, in the Eternal Verbum and this explains how the one which is without any division and sequence becomes *sakhaṇḍa* and *sakrama*. The grammarian states that the Eternal Verbum is the only Reality and sounds or syllables are mere fictions. So, he does not attach any importance to the sequence of sounds; to the contrary, he concentrates on the unitary character of the Eternal Verbum. This concentration or meditation is called *śabda-pūrva-yoga*, a convenient instrument to reach the ultimate goal of life. So, it is said :

> 'Those that reveal the word, viz., sounds or syllables, are like symbols reminding us of the alphabet : they appear as reflections (i.e., they are non-realities); this is to be ascertained through meditation known as *śabda-pūrva-yoga*.'[30]

The commentator while explaining the purport of the above writes :

> The Yogins practising *śabda-pūrva-yoga* as described before meditate on that indivisible word and come to realize that the discrete syllables revealing it in succession are but reflections as in a mirror.

From this it becomes clear that one blessed with *śabda-pūrva-yoga* is fortunate enough to distinguish the Reality from those that are *appearances*; meditation on the unity of the Ultimate Reality, the Word, enables one to realize that the diversity of sounds or syllables and their succession are all figments of imagination.

It needs be mentioned here that Bhartṛhari has not elaborated his view on *śabda-pūrva-yoga* in any one of his *kārikās*. The com., however, mentions it several times :

1. śabdapūrvam......yogaṁ labhate. com. VPS. I. 14
2. tasmāc ca sattānuguṇyamātrāt pratibhākhyāc chabdapūrvayogabhāvanābhyāsākṣepāt pratyastamitasarvavikārollekhamātrāṁ parāṁ prakṛtiṁ pratipadyate. loc. cit.
3. tadabhyāsāc ca śabdapūrvakaṁ yogam adhigamya pratibhām...avabudhya niyatā kṣemaprāptiḥ. com. VPS. I. 123.
4. tasyā eva vāco vyākaraṇena śādhutvajñānalabhyena vā śabdapūrvayogenā'dhigamyate. com. VPS I. 134.

Let us try to understand 2 & 3 :

2 states that an aspirant moves on from *pratibhā* (*paśyantī*) to *Parā Prakṛti* through repeated exercise of *śabda-pūrva-yoga.*

3 mentions that *śabda-pūrva-yoga* enables an aspirant to reach *Paśyantī* and obtain the highest good (*kṣema*).

As far as the text of the *Vākyapadīya* is concerned, we do not find any stage higher than *Paśyantī*. But, if we read 2 & 3 together it is clear that *śabda-pūrva-yoga* leads us to the final goal whether it is *Paśyantī* or *Parā.*

Let us now concentrate on 3 :

Here, we are told that use of chaste forms entitles us to acquire moral power that takes us in the direction of the Ultimate Reality to be identified with it. It is mentioned that as a result of purification of words *apabhraṁśas* are discarded and moral power accrues and *abhyudaya* is attained. Repeated use of chaste words yields more and more *abhyudaya* which initiates *śabda-pūrva-yoga* and through it the aspirant obtains permanent good with the vision of *Paśyantī* dawning upon him.

It may be mentioned that the com. under VPS. I. 14 is a cryptic statement of what is contained in 3 and what we have explained above. There it is said that from the use of chaste forms one develops moral power and approaches the Great Word, elsewhere called the Great Bull and becomes identified with it. The com. runs as follows: sādhuśabdaprayogāc cā'bhivyaktadharmaviśeṣo mahāntam śabdātmānam abhisaṁbhavan vaikaraṇyaṁ (kaivalyam) prāpṇoti.

It is not to be supposed that in the case of use of chaste words it is not necessary to take recourse to *śabda-pūrva-yoga* for purposes of identification of the individual self with the World Soul. Use of chaste words entails moral power and moral power begets *abhyudaya.* Strict adherence to chaste words and their repeated use enables one to acquire more moral power and more *abhyudaya*, ultimately reaching the goal of life through *śabda-pūrva-yoga*.

Let us now turn to 4.

It states that *Paśyantī*, the highest to be achieved in life, is attained through *śabda-pūrva-yoga* coming in the wake of knowledge of chaste words with the help of grammar. A careful and reverent study of grammar acquaints us with chaste words as distinguished from *apabhraṁśas*. This is followed by *śabda-pūrva-yoga* that takes us to the goal.

To sum up : *Śabda-pūrva-yoga* is a necessary aid to the attainment of the goal of life. Patañjali in his *Mahābhāṣya* has introduced a fairly long discussion on the point as to whether religious merit accrues from the knowledge of chaste words or their use or both. The com., as understood and explained above, points out that the ultimate goal is to be reached from the knowledge of chaste words or their use and in either case the spiritual aspirant is to meditate on *śabda-pūrva-yoga* which the commentator under com. on I. 14 describes as follows :

> 'bhedaviṣayatvāt kramasya tatra kramavarṇānugamanaṁ na paśyati tataś cā' satyabhinnaviṣayavyāsaṇgābhāve ekavastūpasaṁhṛtāntaḥkaraṇato yogaṁ labhate.'

Sequence presupposes division. As the Eternal Verbum is indivisible it must be sequenceless. When the mind is concentrated on the unity of the Verbum and turned away from the diversity of sounds that reveal it, it is said to undergo an exercise in *śabda-pūrva-yoga*. To be precise, *śabda-pūrva-yoga* takes us beyond the planes of *vaikharī* and *madhyamā* to the plane of *Paśyantī*. The *modus operandi* in *śabda-pūrva-yoga* is *krama-saṁhāra*, withdrawal of sequence. According to the grammarians, there is sequence in articulate speech (*vaikharī*), there is trace of sequence in mental discourse (*madhyamā*); but, the Eternal Verbum or *Paśyantī* is destitute of all sequence. So, we are to pass on from the gross to the subtle and from the subtle to the more subtle or the subtlest where sequence is entirely eliminated.

Vaikharī represents that stage of manifestation of the Eternal Verbum which is produced in the cavity of the mouth as the breath coming up from within touches the different sources of articulation. It has a purely physical form and is cognised by an external sense-organ. *Vaikharī* is of innumerable variety. When syllables are distinctly pronounced and there is no distortion of any kind, it is called chaste word (*sādhu-śabda*); and, when syllables are not distinct but confused, it is called *apabhraṁśa*. Besides these two, *sādhu* and *apabhrāṁṣa*, the notes of flutes, lutes and drums are also specimens of *vaikharī*. The one most striking feature of *vaikharī* is the sequence of sounds.

Unlike *vaikharī*, *madhyamā* is a less gross manifestation of the Eternal Verbum. It is apprehended by the mind, the internal sense-organ. As it is mental in its constitution it is imperceptible by any external sense-organs. And, as it is more subtle than *vaikharī* in which sequence is clearly exhibited, it seems to be free from all attributes of sequence (*parigṛhītakrame'va*). But, to be strictly precise, the ideas of sequence are associated with it in view of the fact that *madhyamā* follows the course of vital breath (*sūkṣmā prāṇavṛttyanugatā*).

Paśyantī or the Eternal Verbum is one and indivisible into parts. Hence, it is sequenceless. But, the attribute of sequence, which is boldly manifest in *vaikharī* and faintly exhibited in *madhyamā*, is reflected as it were in *Paśyantī* which seems to be endowed with a number of phases. Thus, in the lowest manifestation it appears to be the locus of various objects in their manifold forms; in the second, it assumes a state wherein all forms lie submerged beyond recognition and in the highest it transcends all associations with the diverse objects of the world. Hence, *Paśyantī* manifests objects individually and collectively and yet transcends them and does not manifest them at all. On the empirical plane we come across two classes of words, chaste and unchaste, according as they retain their pristine beauty or lose it by falling off from their original forms. *Paśyantī* transcends both of them. It also transcends the sphere of internal discourse, the plane of *madhyamā*. Thus, *Paśyantī* is the purest state which is completely free from every kind of mixture, homogeneous or heterogeneous. Unlike the other two *Paśyantī* does not follow the movement of vital breath, and, so, it is not influenced by it in any manner. It is immune from division and divested of all attributes of priority and posteriority. As the name suggests, *Paśyantī* is the shining one, the purest of all lights, eternal and ever resplendent. It is described as the immortal lunar digit (*antyā kale'va somasya*) that never fails to diffuse its cool and refreshing rays. Even though it comes into contact with the impurities of the world it remains as pure as ever and therein lies its spiritual character. It may be enquired, however, as to how *Paśyantī* that lies far beyond the empirical plane gets contaminated by impurities. Truth to speak, *Paśyantī* is never contaminated — it is as fresh and pure as ever. Those who fail to distinguish between pure and impure forms, between *sādhu-śabda* and *apabhraṁśa*, may look at *Paśyantī* as mixed up with *apabhraṁśa*, and contaminated. There cannot be any real contamination. There is not the slightest trace of impurity in *Paśyantī*. It is described that as soon as one acquaints oneself with chaste forms through a rigorous and reverent study of grammar, one's mind becomes concentrated and one experiences a determinate communion which is considered to be the step leading to the visualization of *Paśyantī*.[31]

In conclusion, let us state the process of meditation and its culmination in the vision of the Truth and final reunion with it so poetically described in that famous stanza of the Ṛgveda: *Maho devo martyān āviveśa*. The spiritual aspirant reaches the Essence of Speech—the pure luminous Eternal Verbum, which lies beyond the vital plane (*prāṇavṛttim atikrānte*) by withdrawing his mind from external nature (*ātmānaṁ saṁhṛtya*) and fixing it up on his internal nature(*ātmani*). This entails the dissolution of temporal sequence of thought-activity (*krama-saṁhāra-yogena*). The purification of the Verbum results from this and the aspirant enters into it having severed all his ties with the material objective plane. This leads him to the attainment of the internal light and he becomes identical with the undying and undecaying Spirit, the Word-Absolute. Evidently such a conception of the individual self as being merged with the World-Soul, of the unification of the individual consciousness with the Supreme Consciousness is capable of one interpretation, viz., the individual has essential identity with the Absolute beyond which and besides which nothing exists.

And, surely this is monism *in excelsis*.

NOTES

PREFACE

1. varāṭikānveṣaṇāya pravṛttaś cintāmaṇim labdhavān Ś. kau p. 12.

2. prāptyupāyo' nukāraś ca tasya vedo maharṣibhiḥ,
eko 'py anekavartme 'va samāmnātaḥ pṛthak pṛthak. VP. I. 5

3. anādi-nidhanam : without a beginning and an end. In Monistic Vedāntá, there is a list of six held to be *anādi* only; in Nyāya-Vaiśeṣika, *pradhvaṁsābhāva* is described as *ananta* (i.e. *a-nidhana*). But, the Absolute is both *anādi* and *ananta*. It is *samuccaya* that is intended. One should not, therefore, translate this word as 'without a beginning or an end'.

4. *Akṣara* implies pervasion by time and space—this refers to the immanent aspect of the Ultimate Reality; but, *anādi-nidhana* which takes us beyond pervasion by time refers to its transcendent aspect.

5. yāvad brahma viṣṭhitam tāvatī vāk. RV. X. 114. 8

6. maho devo martyān āviveśa. RV. IV. 58. 3

7. VP. I 5.

8. yāṁ sūkṣmāṁ nityām atīndriyāṁ vācam ṛṣayas sākṣātkṛtadharmāṇo mantradṛśaḥ paśyanti, tām asākṣātkṛtadharmabhyo'parebhyaḥ pravedayiṣyamāṇā bilmaṁ samāmananti svapnavṛttam iva dṛṣṭaśrutānubhūtam ācikhyāsanta ity eṣa purākalpaḥ. com. under VP. I. 5- The Rāmāyaṇa describes a situation when the poet blessed with the vision grew restless to express in language what he was feeling within. (Cp. glāyantaḥ = khidyamānāḥ).

9. RV. X. 71. 4

10. akṣare parame vyoman yasmin devā adhi viśve niṣeduḥ RV. I. 164.39

11. Vāk becomes sahasrākṣarā in parama-vyoman, gaurī bubhūvuṣī sahasrākṣarā parame vyoman RV. I. 164.41.

12. It may be submitted that the syntactical construction proposed in the different commentaries on VP. I. 1 is not correct. According to the tradition that we are privileged to inherit, the first five verses forming a *kulaka* describe the transcendent and immanent aspects of the Ultimate Reality. The first half of the opening verse is to be construed as follows : *yad anādinidhanam, brahma, śabdatattvam, akṣaram*; we may compare some of the Mahāvākyas mentioned in the Monistic texts of Vedānta.

13. avyāhatāḥ kalā yasya kālaśaktim upāśritāḥ,
janmādayo vikārāṣ ṣaḍ bhāvabhedasya yonayaḥ. VP. I. 3

14. Kālaśakti or Kāla has nowhere been found in the text of Bhartṛhari to suggest that it is unreal. As such, the objective world that owes its origin to it cannot be unreal. It is only the difference among objects which is a figment of imagination : yannetraḥ pratibhātmā 'yaṁ bhedarūpaḥ pravartate, VP. 1. 119. Mark the suffix '*rūpap*' after '*bheda*' which is added in the sense of '*prāśastya*'. What is intended here is that *bheda* is so patent to our common understanding that it is hardly possible to deny it for all practical purposes. But, even then *bheda* is only a projection of *Śakti* that has her seat in the Eternal Verbum and is described as the fountain-source of the world. It is because of this extremely abstruse nature of the Ultimate Reality in the system of the grammarians that stalwarts like Jayanta-bhaṭṭa, Vācaspatimiśra and Śāntarakṣita have attempted to disover and identify it by offering alternative suggestions that may be consistent with what the grammarian-

philosopher might have in his mind. It is a pity, however, that in later years scholars belonging to different schools of thought started identifying him and his line of thinking with one or another system of their choice with the result that he is sometimes called an exponent of pariṇāma-vāda, vivarta-vāda pratyāsa-vāda or ābhāsa-vāda.

15. api prayoktur ātmānaṁ śabdam antar avasthitam,
prāhur mahāntaṁ ṛṣabhaṁ yena sāyujyam iṣyate. VP. I. 132

16. dvā suparṇā sayujā sakhāyā samānaṁ vṛkṣaṁ pariṣaṣvajāte RV.I 164.20. We are told how Vāk, the daughter of sage Ambhṛṇa, was inspired by her awareness of this union and gave out the well-known Vedic hymn, the *Devīsūkta* as it is called.

17. ekai va vā mahān ātmā devasya. sa sūrya ity ācakṣate. sa hi sarvabhūtātmā. tad uktam ṛṣiṇā sūrya ātmā jagatas tasthuṣaś ca. tadvibhūtayo 'nyā devatāḥ. 14-18

18. yat te rūpaṁ kalyāṇatamaṁ taṁ paśyāmi. yo' sau puruṣaḥ aham asmi. 16

19. It is worthy of observation that in the Chāndogya Upaniṣad besides *sāyujya*, *sālokya* and *sārṣṭi* also have been mentioned. *Sālokya* means living in the same place with the god while *sārṣṭi* means attainment of the powers of God. *Sāmīpya* and *sārūpya* are not mentioned in the Upaniṣads.

20. avaṅ sphoṭāyanasya, Pāṇ. Sū. VI. i. 123
sphoṭāyanas sphoṭapratipādanaparo vaiyākaraṇācāryaḥ. PM. thereunder.

21. kiṁ punar nityaś śabda āhosvit kāryaḥ. MB. Vol. I. P. 54; evaṁ tarhi sphoṭaś śabdo dhvaniś ca śabdaguṇaḥ. op. cit. p. 517; śrotropalabdhir buddhinirgrāhyaḥ prayogeṇā, 'bhijvalita ākāśadeśaś śabdaḥ, op. cit. p. 87

INTRODUCTION

1. dvāv upādānaśabdeṣu śabdau śabdavido viduḥ,
eko nimittaṁ śabdānām aparo'rthe prayujyate. VP. I. 44

Ekaḥ, according to the commentator, means sound. Sound becomes expressive of meaning when it reveals the real word. By *aparaḥ* is meant the real word which is revealed (*prakāśya*) by sound.

Some think that in *śabdānām* the plural is intended; and, so, *śabda* is taken to mean sound. In that case, the meaning would be : *sphoṭa* is the cause of sound—the genesis of sound is the real word. When a person intends to give expression to a meaning, he requisitions the services of appropriate sounds that can reveal *sphoṭa* to the person addressed; and, *sphoṭa*, thus revealed, conveys to him the intended meaning of the speaker. So, *sphoṭa* lying in the mind of the speaker, occasions sounds which, in their turn, reveal *sphoṭa* to the addressee.

Bhartṛhari states that sound and *sphoṭa*, according to the traditional school of thinkers, are different identities. In fact, Patañjali distinguishes the one from the other when he mentions that sound is the attribute of word, i.e., *sphoṭa*. Bhartṛhari, however, records that they may also be viewed as identical; the apparent difference is due to the fact that it is once conceived as the cause and again as the denoter (na ca svagato bhedo'sti, śaktidvayayogāt tu sa eva bhedena pratyavabhāsata ity apare: VPS., p. 103).

2. The half-verse *eko nimittaṁ śabdānām aparo'rthe prayujyate* VP. I. 44 and the half-verse *tadvac chabdo'pi buddhisthaḥ śrutīnāṁ karaṇaṁ pṛthak* VP. I. 46 may be read together. Thus, *ekaḥ* and *buddhisthaḥ śabdaḥ* go together meaning thereby that *sphoṭa*, a self-luminous principle, ever present in the mind, causes sounds to appear so that it is understood by other minds. It is only when sounds have revealed *sphoṭa* to another mind that the latter understands the meaning. Thus, the word present in the mind of the speaker is described as the cause of sound and the word revealed to the addressee by sounds is described as expressive of meaning. The word before it is revealed and the word after it is revealed are identical; they may, however, be looked upon as different in the sense that the one is the cause (of sounds) while the other is the denoter of meaning, one is the manifestor of sounds, the other is manifested by sounds.

We are inclined to think that according to this interpretation, the plural in *śabdānām* is intended to refer to the plurality of sounds. *Sphoṭa* is one and it is the cause of sounds (*śrutīnām*) which in their turn manifest *sphoṭa* that is revealed to the addressee. But, the latter cannot ordinarily distinguish between the two; because, owing to his limitations he realises *sphoṭa* only when it is revealed by sounds, and, therefore, the attributes pertaining to sounds are reflected in *sphoṭa*. In this way, also, *sphoṭa* present in the mind of the speaker may be treated as different from *sphoṭa* revealed to the addressee. The unitary character of *sphoṭa* is clouded by the plurality of sounds reflected in the *sphoṭa*.

3. grāhyatvaṁ grāhakatvañ ca dve śaktī tejaso yathā,
tathai'va sarvaśabdānāṁ ete pṛthag avasthite. VP. I. 55

4. nādasya kramajanmatvān na pūrvo nā'paraś ca saḥ,
akramaḥ kramarūpeṇa bhedavān iva gṛhyate. VP.I, 48

Bhartṛhari freely uses the terms *dhvani*, *varṇa* and *nāda* to mean sound. In Āgama literature *nāda* conveys a special meaning. *Nāda* in yogic and tantrlc exercises occupies a place of some paramount importance. It is described in the *Śāradātilaka* that the first creation of the universe emanates from the *Sakala Parameśvara*. The term *sakala* means 'one endowed with *kalā*' which may be understood as *śakti* or power for all practical purposes. Because *Parmeśvara* in Āgamic philosophy is held to be a dynamic principle with uninterrupted freedom, it is competent to manifest its powers. Prior to the moment of revelation, these powers or *śaktis* remain absorbed in *Parmeśvara* as *kalā*. In the process of creation, *nāda* (or *para-nāda*) comes out of *śakti* and out of *nāda* appears *bindu* or (*para-bindu*). *Nāda* is, therefore, in Āgama literature, the state of *śakti* springing into activity. As such, it must not be confused with sound (*dhvani* or *varṇa*) which is a much later stage in creation.

5. pratibimbam yathā'nyatra sthitaṁ toyakriyāvaśāt,
tatpravṛttim ivā'nveti sa dharmas sphoṭanādayoḥ. VP. I. 49

6. āṇḍabhāvam ivā'panno yaḥ kratuś śabdasaṁjñakaḥ,
vṛttis tasya kriyārūpā bhāgaśo bhajate kramam. VP. I. 51

7. indriyasyai'va saṁskāraś śabdasyai 'vo' bhayasya vā,
kriyate dhvanibhir vādās trayo' bhivyaktivādinām. VP. I. 79

8. ŚV., (śabdanityatā), 51-2; ŚB under MS I. i.5; TS. 2509

9. indriyasyai'va saṁskāras samādhānāñjanādibhiḥ,
viṣayasya tu saṁskāras tadgandhapratipattaye.
cakṣuṣaḥ prāyakāritve tejasā tu dvayor api,
viṣayendriyayor iṣṭas saṁskāras sa kramo dhvaneḥ. VP. I. 80-1

Perception comes in the wake of a contact between the sense-organ and the object to be perceived. The sense-organ lies in the physical organism while the object stays outside. Unless some contact is established between the two, perception does not occur. Philosophers of different schools have tried to explain the nature of contact and their theories are broadly divided into two classes, (i) *prāpyakāritvavāda*, which assumes some sort of actual physical contact and (ii) *aprāpyakāritvavāda*, which denies physical contact and explains the relation in non-physical terms. It is to be noted that there is again a difference of opinion in this matter in respect of particular sense-organs. Bhartṛhari seems to be in favour of *prāpyakāritva* in respect of ocular perception. And in this, he has drawn inspiration from the statements of Patañjali : *apakrāmati tat tasmād darśanam iti.* Kaiyaṭa explains the passage as follows : the ocular organ travels from a person staying in the palace to the object. Nāgeśa elucidates the aforesaid statement as under : the ocular rays like the sun's rays come away from the eyes of the person staying in the palace to reach the object and it is then that the object is visualised. Bhartṛhari states that a person remaining in a dark place can see a jar when his eyes and the jar are both helped by the light. Now, if the eyes have not travelled to the place where the jar is lying, it would not be possible for him to visualize the object as the light does not come to help his eyes. For, a man standing in the light does not see an object lying in the darkness. Hence, it has to be admitted that the light benefits the object as well. It may not be out of place to mention here that Patañjali regards the auditory organ as *aprāpyakārin* and both Kaiyaṭa and Nāgeśa have elaborated this view. It is to be mentioned that Diṅnāga regards the visual organ as *aprāpyakārin.*

10-12 sphoṭarūpāvibhāgena dhvaner grahaṇam iṣyate,
kaiścid dhvanir asaṁvedyas svatantro'nyaḥ prakāśakaḥ. VP. I. 82; com thereunder.

13. yathā 'nuvākaś śloko vā soḍhatvam anugacchati,
āvṛttyā na tu sa granthaḥ pratyāvṛtti nirūpyate.
pratyayair anupākhyeyair grahaṇānuguṇais tathā,
dhvaniprakāśite śabde svarūpam avadhāryate. VP. I. 83-4
Also, com. on SS.18

14. nādair āhitabījāyām antyena dhvaninā saha,
āvṛttaparipākāyāṁ buddhau śabdo'vadhāryate. VP. I.85

15. yathai'va darśanaiḥ pūrvair dūrāt santamase'pi vā,
anyathākṛtya viṣayām anyathai'vādhyavasyati. VP. I. 89.
Also SS. 19 and com. thereunder.

16. vyajyamāne tathā vākye vākyābhivyaktihetubhiḥ,
bhāgāvagraharūpeṇa pūrvaṁ buddhiḥ pravartate. VP. I. 91

17. dhvanayas sadṛśātmāno viparyāsasya hetavaḥ,
upalambhakam eve'ṣṭaṁ viparyāsasya kāraṇam SS. 20.
Also, com. on YSB.III.17

18. yathā'dyasaṁkhyāgrahaṇam upāyaḥ pratipattaye,
saṁkhyāntarāṇāṁ bhede'pi tathā śabdāntaraśrutiḥ. VP. I. 88

19. yathā'nupūrvīniyamo vikāre kṣīrabījayoḥ,
tathai'va pratipattṝṇāṁ niyato buddhiṣu kramaḥ. VP. I. 92
20. asataś cā'ntarāle yāñ chabdān astī'ti manyate,
pratipattur aśaktis sā grahaṇopāya eva saḥ. VP. I.86. Also, SS. 153-57
21. nityaparyāyī siddhaśabdaḥ. M.B., Vol.I., p. 56
22. anekavyaktyabhivyaṅgyā jātis sphoṭa iti smṛtā,
kaiścid vyaktaya evā'syā dhvanitvena prakalpitāḥ. VP. I. 94
23. na cā'nityeṣv abhivyaktir niyamena vyavasthitā,
āśrayaír api nityānāṁ jātīnāṁ vyaktīr iṣyate. VP.I. 96
24. deśādibhiś ca sambandho dṛṣṭaḥ kāyavatām iha,
deśabhedavikalpe'pi na bhedo dhvaniśabdayoḥ. VP. I. 97
25. sphoṭasyā 'bhinnakālasya dhvanikālānupātinaḥ,
grahaṇopādhibhedena vṛttibhedaṁ pracakṣate.
svabhāvabhedān nityatve hrasvadīrghaplutādiṣu,
prākṛtasya dhvaneḥ kālaś śabdasye 'ty upacaryate.
varṇasya grahaṇe hetuḥ prākṛto dhvanir iṣyate,
sthitibhede nimittatvaṁ vaikṛtaḥ pratipadyate.
śabdasyo'rdhvam abhivyakter vṛttibhede tu vaikṛtāḥ,
dhvanayas samupohante sphoṭātmā tair na bhidyate. VP. I. 75-8
26. tasmād abhinnakāleṣu varṇavākyapadādiṣu,
vṛttikālas svakālaś ca nādabhedād vibhajyate. VP.I.102
27. deśavyāptisāmānyād alpatvamahatve śabdasyo'pacaryete. lokaprasiddher vā lokaprasiddhir eva hi sarvatra vyavasthākāraṇam. śabdo' tra dhvaniḥ. sa ca dvividha uttarottaraśabdānāṁ kāraṇarūpa ādyaḥ kāryarūpa uttaraś ca. tatrā' dyas sphoṭavyañjakas sphoṭa eva vā. tasya kāraṇarūpasya kāryārambhaśaktis sāmarthyaṁ nimittabhedād bhidyate yathā bherīdaṇḍābhighātajasya kāryaparamparā dūram anupatati lohakaṁsābhighātajas tu pratyāsannadeśadīrghakāla-grāhyam avicchedenā'rabhate, tad āha paras tv iti. tatrā'dyaḥ prākṛtaḥ paro vaikṛta iti bodhyam. com. on VP.I.104
28. vāyor aṇūnāṁ jñānasya śabdatvāpattir iṣyate. VP.I.108
29. labdhakriyaḥ prayatnena vaktur icchānuvartinā,
sthāneṣv abhihato vāyuś śabdatvaṁ pratipadyate. V.P.I.109
Also : tathā ca śikṣākārā āhur vāyur āpadyate śabdatām. ŚB.pp.90-1
30. na ca vāyavīyān avayavān śabde sataḥ pratyabhijānīmaḥ. syāc ced evaṁ sparśanena upalabhāmahe. loc. cit.
31. N.Ku.II. pp.33-4
32. There are texts which seem to suggest that sounds are products of air. But, we think that these texts can be consistently explained if air is supposed to function as a manifesting medium (*vyañjaka*) and sounds are regarded as the properties of ether.
33. For the Jaina conception of word, see PNT. III. 9 and the com. RKT thereunder.

CHAPTER ONE

1. parimāṇasya svasamānajātīyasvotkṛṣṭaparimāṇajanakatvaniyamāt. SM. under BP., 15
2. avayavinyūnaparimāṇatvād avayavānāṁ paramamahatvāc ca varṇānāṁ tadanupapatteḥ. TB., p. 2

3. ākāśasya tu vijñeyaś śabdo vaiśeṣiko guṇaḥ. BP., 44
4. samavāyikāraṇatvaṁ dravyasyai've'ti vijñeyam. op. cit., 23
5. This theory has been discussed in the introduction.
6. asamavāyikāraṇanāśasya dravyanāśajanakatvāt. Din. on SM. under BP., 18
7. vāyavīyāvayavārabdhavarṇavādinām apy āśutaravināśaśīlatayā varṇānāṁ parasparam asahabhuvām asambaddhānām avayavavyārambhāsambhavāt, na khalv ete kramabhāvino 'vayavinaṁ vā tadasamavāyikāraṇaṁ vā vyatiṣaṅgaṁ bibhrati. abibhrāṇāś ca katham avayavā vyatiṣaktā vā. ekadravyasya ca kāryadravyasyā' nupapatteḥ dravyavināśakāraṇadvayābhāvena kṛtakanityatvaprasaṅgāt. TB. pp. 2-8
8. VP. I. 84
9. pade na varṇā vidyante varṇesv avayavā iva,
vākyāt padānām atyantaṁ praviveko na kaścana. VP. I. 73

Also, vākyasphoṭo 'tiniṣkarṣe tiṣṭhatī'ti matasthitiḥ. VBS., 61

Also, varṇasphoṭādīnām ākāṅkṣānivartakatvābhāvād avāstavatvaṁ śāstrīyaprakriyānirvāhāya paraṁ siddhānte tatsvīkāraḥ pāramārthikatvaṁ tu vākyasphoṭasya. VBSD. under VBS., 61

10. *Ūha* :— prakṛtāv āmnātasya mantrasya vikṛtau samavetārthatvāya taducitapadāntaraprakṣepeṇa pāṭha ūhaḥ. RVB., p. 21

Patañjalī in his *Mahābhāṣya*, has mentioned the manifold importance of the study of Sanskrit Grammar. He says that in the Vedic hymns no word is found to have been used in various inflexions and conjugations, as the case may be, to suit various practical purposes for which they are enjoined. It is, therefore, that necessary changes in the wording are made according to circumstances. This change in the wording is called *ūha*. And, it is for this purpose that a knowledge of the principles of grammar is necessary. Kaiyaṭa explains the point by saying that in a sacrifice in honour of the Sun-god, the term '*agnaye*' in the expression, *agnaye tvā juṣṭaṁ nirvapāmi*, should be substituted by the term '*sūryāya*.'

Prasaṅga :— When a particular thing which is prescribed in connection with a particular sacrifice, is incidentally prescribed in connection with another we have a case of *prasaṅga* : anyoddeśena anyadīyasyā 'pi sahānuṣṭhānaṁ prasaṅgaḥ. JNM, p, 666

Tantra :—When a subordinate sacrificial act (*aṅga-yāga*) is prescribed only in connection with a number of principal sacrifices, we have a case of *tantra* : ubhayoddeśena sakṛd anuṣṭhānaṁ tantram. loc. cit.

11. yatas sphoṭapakṣe hi niravayavaṁ vākyaṁ niravayavasya vākyārthasya vācakam, avayavās tu padātmakā varṇātmakāś ca mṛṣābhūtā itī'ṣyate. tataś ca padatadavayavāśritasyo 'hāder mahāvākyāvayavāntaravākyārthaprayājādyāśritasya prasaṅgatantrādeś co' ttaratra vicāryamāṇasya mṛṣātvaṁ syāt. atas tatsatyatāsiddhyarthaṁ sphoṭanirākaraṇam iti na niṣphalam. Prabhā under ŚB. I. i. 5, p. 49

12. The sacrifice in which the details of the ceremony are described and according to which other sacrifices are performed is called the principal sacrifice while the latter are called derivative sacrifices. Vide, MBP., Vol. I, p. 20

13. Vide, ŚV (sphoṭāvāda).

Also, durvidagdhair avakṣipte darśane padadarśinām,
yathāgamaṁ yathāprajñaṁ nyāyaleśo nidarśyate. SS., 2

14. nirastabhedaṁ padatattvam ekam,
vyadarśi yuktyāgamasaṁśrayeṇa. SS., 36

Maṇḍana's sole object was to criticise Kumārila who apprehended that if the doctrine of *sphoṭa* be accepted, words (*pada*) would be meaningless. Maṇḍana has, therefore, discussed *pada-sphoṭa* purposely; or, how else he could have mentioned *vākya-sphoṭa*. SS., 29

15. tasmād anityānāṁ varṇānāṁ eva vācakatvaṁ pratiṣṭhāpanīyañ ca parākramaṇīyaś sphoṭaḥ. NM., p. 367

16. Cp. The Joint Method of Agreement and Difference in western logic. To determine causal relation, this method is often resorted to by Sanskrit logicians and writers. The rhetoricians have laid down as a rule that in order to distinguish between *śabda-guṇa*, and *artha-guṇa*, between *śabda-doṣa* and *artha-doṣa* and between *śabdā-laṅkāra* and *arthā-laṅkāra* we should apply this method. SD., p. 429

17. ataś śravaṇagrahaṇatā eva śabdalakṣaṇaṁ nyāyyam. vārṇā eva ce 'daṁ śabdalakṣaṇam anupatantī' ty abhidheyadhīhetubhāvam anupayanto' pi lokaprasiddhes ta eva śabdāḥ. SS., p. 13

18. According to the grammarians, *sphoṭa* may be perceived through the mind. Vācaspati in his *Tattvabindu* states that *sphoṭa* or *śabdatattva* is cognised by means of mental perception : tad eva hi sarvajanīnamānasapratyakṣapravedanīyaprayatnabhedabhinnanānādhvanipratyekavyañjanīyaṁ tattvam TB., p. 8. Śaṅkarācārya, quotes the view of those who support the theory of *sphoṭa* by saying that it is cognised by perception : na kalpayāmy ahaṁ sphoṭaṁ pratyakṣam eva tv enam avagacchāmi. Śār. Bh., p. 327 It should be observed, however, that Jayanta describes *sphoṭa* as an entity which is cognised through the auditory organ : paramārthatas tu śrautre pratyaye pratibhāsamānaḥ. NM., p. 371 Thus, we find that it is unanimously believed that *sphoṭa* is cognised by perception. But, we must admit that we do not subscribe to Jayanta's views when he says that *sphoṭa* is perceived by the auditory organ; for, had it been so, the charges generally levelled against the theory by the Naiyāyikas, namely, that it is neither perceived nor inferred, would be irrelevant.

19. yadi hi pratyuccāraṇaṁ gavādivyaktivad anyā anyā varṇavyaktayaḥ pratīyeran tata ākṛtinimittaṁ pratyabhijñānaṁ syāt, na tv etad asti. Śār. Bh., p. 325. Also, *Bhāmatī* thereunder.

20. saty api vā tathāvidhe sāmastye nā'sty evā' rthapratītiḥ. NM., p. 368

21. asahabhāvitvād eva anubhūyamānatayā'py avayavabhāvaḥ parāsto veditavyaḥ TB., p. 8

N. B. : The discussion on the possibility or otherwise of obtaining the cognition of the aggregate of letters finds an echo in Jayanta; see, NM. pp. 367-8

22. athavā vāsanai 'vā' stu saṁskāras sarva eva hi,
dṛḍhajñānagṛhītārthe saṁskāro 'stī' ti manyate. ŚV., (sphoṭavāda) 99

Also, pūrvapūrvavarṇajanitasaṁskārasahito 'ntyo varṇaḥ vācakaḥ. NM., p. 368

23. yo hi yadgocarānubhavayonis saṁskāras, sa tatrai 'va dhiyam

ādhatta iti tasya svabhāvaḥ. yady anyasminn apy ādadhāti. kiñcid evai 'kam anubhūya sarvas sarvaṁ artham vijānīyāt. api ca saṁskāra iti ca vāsane' ti ca bhāvane 'ti ca prācīnānubhavajanitātmanas sāmarthyabhedam eva smṛtijñānaprasavahetum ācakṣate, na cā 'syai' vā 'rthapratyayaprasavaśaktiś śakyā kalpayitum. TB., p. 6

24. eṣā prācīnajñānasya śaktir ātmani ca tiṣṭhaty athavā 'tmanaś śaktiḥ pūrvajñānena janyate. Gop. under SS., 7

25. śakteś śaktyantarāyogas tatra saty apy adarśanam,
vilakṣaṇasyopajano nā 'viśeṣāc ca kāraṇāt. SS., 7

26. tad idam asamañjasam iva lakṣyate. SS., 52

27. yo hi sphoṭaṁ kalpayati tena sphoṭasyā 'rthapratipādanaśaktir api kalpanīye'ti kalpanāgauravam. ubhayasiddhasya saṁskārasya sāmarthya-kalpanāyāṁ tu lāghavam asti.

yady api smṛtihetutvaṁ saṁskārasya vyavasthitam,
kāryāntare 'pi sāmarthyaṁ na tasya pratihanyate. NK., p. 271

28. na khalu kramabhede 'pi pratyekam akṣaropalambhaprabhāvitās saṁskārāḥ parasparam atiśerate. Gop. under SS., 7

29. Smṛtidvāreṇa tarhy arthapratyāyako' sau bhaviṣyati. NM. p. 368

30. smṛtisamārohiṇo varṇā vācakās tan na gauravam iti cen na. kramākramaviparītakramāṇāṁ tatrā 'viśeṣeṇā' rthadhīsamutpādanaprasaṅgāt. TB., p. 7

31. tato rājā jārā kapiḥ pika ityādiṣu viśeṣapratipattir na syāt. Śār. Bh., p. 327

32. pratyekapadapadārthānubhavabhāvitabhāvanānicayalabdhajanma-smṛtadarpaṇārūḍhā varṇamālā ity anye. TB., p. 2

Also, antyavarṇe ca vijñāte sarvasaṁskārakāritam, smaraṇaṁ
yaugapadyena sarveṣv anye pracakṣate. Śv., (sphoṭavāda); 112

also; the introductory com. to SS., 8,pp. 58-61

33. atha vā kramopalabdheṣv api varṇeṣu mānasam anuvyavasāyarūpam akhilavarṇaviṣayaṁ saṅkalanājñānaṁ yad upajāyate tad arthapratyāyanāṅgaṁ bhaviṣyati. dṛśyate ca vinaśvareṣv api padārthāntareṣu kramānubhūteṣu yugapad anuvyavasāyo mānasaś śatam āmrāṇi bhakṣitavān devadatta iti. NM., p. 376

34. yathā pūrvavarṇajanitasaṁskārasahito 'ntyavarṇa iti tatrabhavatā mīmāṁsābhāṣyakṛtā varṇitaṁ tathā vā varṇānām arthapratyāyakatvam astu. loc. cit.

35. SS., pp. 58-63

36. The force of the term '*samanantara*' (immediately) in the com. of SS., p. 61, should be carefully studied.

37. asamprāptaniranvayaniruddhayor viśeṣābhāvād ity uktam. SS., p. 66

38. ekopalabdhau tu yaugapadyān nā 'nupūrvīko viśeṣaḥ. loc. cit.

39. svato varṇā nityatayā vibhutayā vā na deśanibandhanaṁ nā 'pi kālanibandhanaṁ parāparabhāvam anupatantī 'ti prakhyānanibandhana eṣa samupāśrīyate. loc. cit.

40. yāvanto yādṛśā ye ca yadarthapratipādane, varṇāḥ
prajñātasāmarthyās te tathai'vāvabodhakāḥ. ŚV., Sphoṭavāda 69

41. SS., pp. 74-5

42. brūyāt padavākyayor ekatvam antareṇa kathaṁ padavākyārtha-

pratītir ekarūpā bhaved iti so 'yam atīva mugdhālāpaḥ. pratītibhedābhedau hi viṣayabhedābhedāv anurudhyete no 'pāyabhedābhedau, NM., PP. 382-3

43. śrautre pratyaye pratibhāsamānaḥ pratyakṣa eva sphoṭaḥ. NM., p. 371

44. Indian logicians lay it down that a definition must be neither wide (*ativyāpta*), nor narrow (*avyāpta*) nor wholly absurd (*asambhava*). If 'man' be defined as a biped animal, the definition is said to be wide for the denotation of the term in question is increased. And, if the definition happens to decrease the denotation, it is said to be narrow. Again, if we define an object in such a way that the definition does not enable us to understand it at all, on the contrary, it is applicable to another object quite different from it, our definition is said to be absurd. (Cp. C. Read, p. 377)

45. yeno 'ccāritena sāsnālāṅgūlakakudakhuraviṣāṇināṁ sampratyayo bhavati sa śabdaḥ. MB., Vol. I, p. 16. Maṇḍana summarises the idea in the third *kārikā* of his work : arthāvasāyaprasavanimittaṁ śabda iṣyate.

46. anyo 'pi vācakas saṅgatisaṁvedanasamayataś ca puraś śravaṇendriyāvaseyo' pi na śabda iti nigadyate, paścāc ca tatho' cyate. SS. p. 19

47. MB., Vol. I, p. 12, and Pradīpa thereunder.

48. dravyaṁ nāma tat. MB., Vol. I, p. 14

49. bhinnendriyagrāhyatvān na dravyaṁ śabda iti pratītam, api tu dravyam iti. loc. cit.

50. loc. cit.

51. SS., pp. 15-9 and Gop. thereunder.

52. Mill, *System of Logic*, Vol. I, p. 379

53. anyathāsiddhiśūnyasya niyatā pūrvavartitā,
kāraṇatvaṁ bhavet. ...... BP. 16

The term *anyathāsiddha* requires elucidation. Logicians have spoken of the fivefold varieties of *anyathāsiddhi*. First, an essential attribute (or attributes) which determines the cause of an effect is said to be *anyathāsiddha*; and, it is not, therefore, regarded as the cause. For instance, 'staff' determined by 'staff-hood' is the cause of 'pot'; so, 'staff-hood' should not be regarded as the cause of the pot. Secondly, a phenomenon the agreement in presence and absence of which in relation to an effect is only possible through the medium of another (the real cause) is also *anyathāsiddha*. The 'form' of 'staff' is not the cause of 'pot' in view of the fact that its agreement in presence and absence with 'pot' is possible through the medium of 'staff' only and not by itself. Thirdly, an *anyathāsiddha* is one which is known to be the antecedent of another phenomenon only when it is known to be the antecedent of a different one. The 'sky', for example, is not the cause of 'pot' as we know that the 'sky' contributes to the production of 'pot' only when it is known that it is the inherent cause of 'word' (*śabda*). Fourthly, what happens to be the cause of the cause of an effect is also *anyathāsiddha*. The 'father' of the pot-maker cannot be the cause of 'pot' made by his son. Lastly, anything other than the least antecedent which suffices to produce the consequent, is regarded as *anyathāsiddha*. It may be a fact that at the time when a pot is made, a cow is present on the spot; but, it will not be justified to say that the animal contributes to the production of the pot and should be looked upon as its cause.

CHAPTER TWO

1. yasyā 'navayavas sphoṭo vyajyate varṇabuddhibhiḥ,
so' pi paryanuyogeṇa nai 'vā 'nena vimucyate. ŚV., (sphoṭavāda), 84.

2. tad yathā ratnaparīkṣiṇaḥ punaḥ punā ratnasvarūpaṁ vīkṣamāṇasya ratnadarśanāni pratyekaṁ ratnasvarūpam avagāhamānāny api na sahasai 'va samānāsamānajātīyavyāvṛttaṁ ratnatattvam avabhāsayanti, kintu pañcaṣadarśanajanitabhāvanāsacivacetolabdhajanmani carame cetasi cakāsti ratnatattvam. TB., pp. 4-5; also, yathā ratnaparīkṣakāṇāṁ......ratnatattvam. NM., p. 370; also, yathā ratnaparīkṣiṇaḥ...ratnatattvam. SS., p. 13

3. pratyayair anupākhyeyair grahaṇānuguṇais tathā,
dhvaniprakāśite śabde svarūpam avadhāryate. VP. I. 84

4. pratyakṣajñānaniyatā vyaktāvyaktāvabhāsitā,
mānāntareṣu grahaṇam athavā nai' va hi grahaḥ. SV., (sphoṭavāda) 23

5. arthaś ca śabdapratyayāvaseyas sphoṭātmā tu pratyakṣavedanīya iti niravadyam. SS., p. 171

6. dhvaner udānasya vāgindriyābhighātino yaḥ pariṇatibhedo varṇātmā. com. on YSV., p. 140

7. *Upādhi* is one of those marks that distinguishes an object from others. Logicians recognise three distinguishing marks, viz., *viśeṣaṇa*, *upādhi* and *upalakṣaṇa*. A *viśeṣaṇa* is one which is related to the substantive (*viśeṣya*) and is present in the substantive at the time when it distinguishes the same from others. For instance, in such expressions as '*vidyāvān puruṣaḥ*' (a learned man), *vidyā* (learning) is related to *puruṣa* (man) and the latter is in actual possession of *vidyā* when he is called *vidyāvān*. Hence, *vidyā* is said to be a *viśeṣaṇa*. A *upādhi*, on the other hand, is only present in the substantive but not related to it. The sense-organ for auditory perception is defined as the portion of the sky which is determined by the outer part of the ear (*karṇa-śaṣkulī*). Here, the ear cannot be related to the sky but, being present, distinguishes the particular sky from others (e.g. *ghaṭākāśa, paṭākāśa*). The well-known example of a *upādhi* in Indian Philosophy is the crimson *japā* flower (*hibiscus rosasinensis*), which contributes to the reddishness in the crystal beside it. Vardhamāna's com. on NKu. III, p. 38 and Yogendranātha's com. on AS., Vol. II, p. 587, *re*: *pratipannopādhi*. A *upalakṣaṇa*, however, is neither related to the substantive nor is required to be present in it. It distinguishes the substantive at a time when it is not present itself. A man, for instance, once went to a house on the top of which there sat a crow. But, when he is later on required to distinguish the same house from other houses, he does so by remembering the fact that he saw a crow on the top of that house. The crow is not present there at the time when he remembers the house. Mark the following observation on this point : upādhiś ca kāryānanvayī vyāvartako vartamānaś ca; viśeṣaṇañ ca kāryānvayi vyāvartakaṁ vartamānam. VPar., p. 97. And, we may add : upalakṣaṇañ ca kāryānanvayi vyāvartakam avartamānañ ca.

8. yathā kṛpāṇamaṇidarpaṇādivyañjakabhedena śyāmadīrghādi rūpaṁ vadanasya. nādātmako hi śabdo vīṇāveṇumṛdaṅgapaṭahādivyañjakabhedena nānātvam upagacchati. NM., p. 370

9. varṇāc ca samāropitadīrghatvādidharmabhājaḥ pāramārthikārtha-

dhībhedopalambhāt, tathā hi laukikā naga iti girim upadiśanti nāga iti hastinam. TB. p. 5

10. atha gaur ity atra kaś śabdaḥ. gakāraukāravisarjanīyā iti bhagavān upavarṣaḥ. ŚB., on MS.,I.i. 5

11. smṛter api kṣaṇikatvāt. op. cit.

12. This *saṁskāra* should be clearly distinguished from *vāsanā* which is also so called: mā bhūd eṣa jñānaprasavas smaraṇanimittaṁ saṁskāra api tu yāgādikarmabhedopapādita iva svargādinimittam apūrvābhidhānaḥ. SS., p. 86; also ko nu khalv ayaṁ saṁskāro 'bhimata āyuṣmataḥ kiṁ smṛtibījam anyo vā prokṣaṇādibhya iva vrīhyādeḥ. TB., p. 6

13. pūrvavarṇajanitasaṁskārasahito 'ntyo varṇaḥ pratyāyaka ity adoṣaḥ ŚB., p. 46

14. Nir. I. 1

15. na hi laukikavacanam anupapannam ity etāvatā pratyakṣādibhir anavagamyamāno 'rthaś śaknoty upagantum...śāstrakāravacanam apy alam imam artham apramāṇakam upapādayitum. ŚB., p. 47

16. svavyāpāravyavāyo 'pi sarvasminn eva kārake,
dṛṣṭo vyāpāra īdṛk ca śabdasye 'ty avyapetatā. ŚV., (sphoṭavāda) 125 and 128; also, na hi svavyāpāravyavāyaḥ kārakāṇāṁ kārakatām vihanti. SS., p. 90

17. na gauṇaś śabdo mā bhūd iti pratyakṣādibhir anavagamyamāno 'rthaś śakyaḥ parikalpayitum. ŚB., p. 48

18. śabdakalpanāyāṁ sā ca śabdakalpanā ca. loc. cit.

19. pūrvanādāhitasaṁskārasahitāntimanādābhivyaṅgyas sphoṭa ity avaśyam aṅgīkartavyam iti tulyā saṁskārakalpanā. Ś. Dīp., p. 96

20. api ca tārkikāṇām anumānapriyatvāt tatparitoṣāye 'dam anumānam abhyadhāyi na paramārthataḥ. NM., p. 371

21. aho vatā 'sya svapakṣadṛṣṭipakṣapāto yad bahutarādṛṣṭasambhārakalpanākleśam api na cetayate. TB., p. 6

22. The *raison d'etre* is this : The knowledge of the attribute is required to be obtained prior to the knowledge of the qualified. viśiṣṭabuddhau viśeṣaṇajñānasya kāraṇatvāt. SM. under BP. 58

23. na cā 'ntyavarṇamātrasya puras sambandhavedanam,
akṣavartmātivṛttatvāt saṁskārasya na tadvataḥ. SS., 13

24. yat punar avādi prathamavarṇabuddhivelāyām iva vyaktaṁ sphoṭatattvam uttarottarabuddhibhir atiśayitatarapratyayatāṁ nīyate ratnatattvavad iti sa eva viṣama upanyāsaḥ. ratnasya hi sāvayavatvāt prathamapratyayāviṣayīkṛtasūkṣmatarāvayavaviśeṣāgrāhiṇām uttarottarapratyayānām asti tatrāvakāśaḥ. sphoṭas tu varṇasvarūpavad anaṁśa iti tatsvarūpasarvasvam ādyenai 'va varṇena vyaktaṁ kim idānīm anye varṇā kariṣyanti. NM., p. 378

25. It may be noted here that the objection which Jayanta has raised, has suggested itself to him from an observation of Kumārila who asserts that letters are indivisible units, and, as such, they will be either clearly and completely cognised or not cognised at all; the question of partial cognition cannot arise in the case of indivisible entities. Arguing on this line, Jayanta advances his objection to the gradual revelation of *sphoṭa* which the grammarian describes as indivisible. ŚV., (sphoṭavāda 10)

26. ratnatattvadṛṣṭānto 'py ayuktaḥ;........., tadvad atra sphoṭe, pūrva-

pūrvābhivyaktyaviṣayāṇām abhivyaktiviṣayāṇāñ ca viśeṣāṇā m abhāvāc ca. VKP., p. 331

27. YSV. III. 17; also Vācaspati's com. thereunder.

28. yady api kāryātmanā udricyate tathā 'pi yat svarūpaṁ pūrṇatvaṁ paramātmabhāvaṁ tan na jahāti. BB, p. 729

29. atyantaviviktayor dharmadharmiṇor mithyājñānanimittas satyānṛte mithunīkṛtyā 'ham idaṁ mame 'dam iti naisargiko 'yam lokavyavahāraḥ. Śār. Bh., pp. 17-8

30. YS. III. 17

CHAPTER THREE

1. tatra varṇapadavākyabhedena sphoṭas tridhā. tatrā 'pi jātivyaktibhedena punaṣ ṣoḍhā. khaṇḍapadasphoṭo' khaṇḍavākyasphoṭaś ce 'ti saṅkalanayā 'ṣṭau sphoṭāḥ.' PLM., p. 1

2. yathā 'nandavalyāṁ śuddhabrahmajñānārthaṁ annamayaprāṇamayamanomayavijñānamayānandamayeti pañcasu kośeṣv apāramārthikabrahmatvapratipādanam upāyaḥ. SC., p. 1

3. ata eva sphuṭyate vyajyate varṇais sphoṭo varṇābhivyaṅgyas sphuṭati sphuṭībhavaty asmād artha iti sphoṭo' rthapratyāyaka iti sphoṭaśabdārtham ubhayathā nirāha. SDS., p. 112

4. Grammatically, a *sthānin* is one which is not actually used in a place where it has every right to be used (prasakto 'py aprayujyamānaḥ). For instance, when *dadhi+atra* yields *dadhy-atra* according to the rules of assimilation, it is said that the last letter in *dadhi*; i.e., '*i*'; is the *sthānin* whereas the '*y*' which replaces it, is called the *ādeśa.*

5. An *adhikāra sūtra* is a governing rule which exerts a directing influence over other rules. For instance, Pāṇ. Sū. VIII. i.1 is an *adhikāra sūtra*; for, it has a governing influence over the sūtras VIII. i. 2-10. This governing influence is of three kinds : (i) *gaṅgāpravāha,* (ii) *siṁhāvalokita* and (iii) *maṇḍūkapluti.*

6. Elision means *absence* : adarśanaṁ lopaśabdārtham āha. Cp. Pāṇ.Sū., I. i. 60

7. ādeśinām api tattadvaiyākaraṇais svecchayā bhinnānām abhyupagamāt. VBS., pp. 418-19

8. evañ ca sthāny eva vācako lāghavāt na tvā'deśo gauravād iti tārkikoktam apāstam. SC., p. 1

9. vastutas tu samabhivyāhārasya vācakatve tadghaṭakanānāvarṇānām avacchedakatāyāṁ gauravam. varṇānāṁ vācakatve tu uktānupūrvyā ekasyā eva tattvam iti lāghavasyai'va vinigamakatvam iti bodhyam. VBSD., p. 421

10. The *Nirukta* defines a verb (*ākhyāta*) as one in which the operation (*bhāva*) is prominent. The term 'prominent' requires elucidation. It has been laid down that in the case of verbal knowledge, the operation must appear as substantive and never as an attribute. And, this is the significance of the term 'prominent.' According to the grammarians, the operation called *bhāvanā* refers to the following operations in the case of *pacati* (cooking): applying heat to the pot, placing it on the furnace and the like. According to the Naiyāyikas, the term means the exertion (*kṛti* or *prayatna*) which is instrumental in bringing about the operation. The difference

between the two views is that *bhāvanā*, according to the grammarians, means the operation which is caused by the exertion while the Naiyāyikas regard the exertion itself as *bhāvanā*. In the opinion of the Naiyāyikas, exertion is denoted by *-tiṅ* suffixes while the sense of the nominative is denoted by *kṛt* suffixes.

The Mīmāṁsakas define *bhāvanā* as the operation on the part of the *causer* (*prayojaka-kartṛ*) which serves to help the *one to be produced* (*i.e.*, the exertion of the doer) in the matter of its production. (bhāvanā nāma bhavitur bhavanānukūlabhāvakavyāpāraviśeṣaḥ, NP., p. 2). And, this *bhāvanā* has been divided into *śābdī* and *ārthī*, according as it pertains to the word-element or the sense-element respectively. The former has been defined as the operation of the *causer* which causes the exertion of the performer of sacrifices. The verb comprises the root and the suffix. The latter is marked by two attributes : (i) that it is an *ākhyāta* (verb) and (ii) that it is a *liṅ*. It may be noted that we are dealing here with Vedic injunctions. Now, in the Vedas, it is from the use of *liṅ* that we know that a particular action is enjoined to be performed. Hence, it is *liṅ* that serves to express *bhāvanā* which is known to be *śābdī* pertaining as it does to the form of *liṅ*. It has been maintained that *śābdī bhāvanā* cannot be complete unless the following three points are known : what is to be produced by the operation (*śābdī-bhāvanā*), how and by whom. It is asserted that the *ākhyāta* element in the suffix answers to the first part by saying that the exertion of the doer is produced by the operation on the part of the causer. And, this exertion of the doer is said to be *ārthī bhāvanā*. We may observe the *bhāvanā* as conceived by the Naiyāyikas, resembles *ārthī bhāvanā* of Mīmāṁsakas. It may be discussed here that Laugākṣi-bhāskara in his *Artha-saṁgraha* has put the term *vyāpāra* in the definition of *ārthī bhāvanā*; but, it has been clearly stated in the *Kaumudī* that this term *vyāpāra* means exertion (*prayatna*). A Sam., pp. 22.39. In the end, we like to point out that the term *bhāvanā* has been used by the Bhāṭṭa school of Mīmāṁsakas; the Prābhākara school has used the term *niyoga* in its place.

11. śuddhabrahmajñānāya sarvabahirbhūtānnamayakośavad akhaṇḍa-vākyasphoṭabodhanāya varṇasphoṭaḥ SC., p. 5

12. athā' deśā vācakāś cet padasphoṭas tataḥ punaḥ. VBS. 64

13. The term *prātipadika* technically means a word or a letter which is neither a root nor a suffix but carries some sense. (Pāṇ. Sū. I.ii. 45). Moreover, a *prātipadika* is one which is formed by the addition of a *kṛt* or a *taddhita* suffix or happens to be a compound word (op. cit., I. ii. 46).

14. Pāṇ. Sū. I. iv. 14

15. When two rules of equal strength may be operated for the same purpose, the one coming later in the order of sūtras in the *Aṣṭādhyāyī* is given preference: yatra dvau prasaṅgāv anyārthāv ekasmin yugapat prāpnutas sa tulyabalavirodho vipratiṣedhaḥ. Kāś. p. 61. According to Pāṇ. Sū. VIII ii. 66, both VIII. iii. 14 and VI.I. 114 may be applied in the case of *manas+rathaḥ*. And, had it not been for the fact that VIII. iii. 14 is *asiddha*, the elision sanctioned by the same would have happened by the above dictum. But, the term *param* in the dictum is differently interpreted by Patañjali who says that the term *param* does

not mean 'what comes next' but means 'what is desired'; and, he refers to such expressions as 'paraṁ dhāma gataḥ' where '*param*' is used in the latter sense. Kaiyaṭa says that what is desired and what is not so, should be understood in the light of the explanations of the authorities (specially Patañjali) on the subject under consideration; iṣṭāniṣṭavibhāgaś ca vyākhyānād bodhyaḥ, MB., Vol. II, p. 207. In the context, Haradatta has followed the second explanation of the term.

16. Kielhorn translates the injunction thus : What is taught in a rule the application of which occasioned by the combination of two things, does not become the cause of the destruction of that combination.

It is argued on the strength of this injunction that the '*a*' in *rāma* should not have been lengthened in the case of *rāmāya*, the dative singular of *rāma*. For, here, the substitute '*ya*' in the place of '*ṅe*' ought not to have caused the application of Pāṇ. Sū. VII. iii. 102 on the ground that '*ya*' owes its substitution to the combination of the base *rāma* ending in short '*a*' with the termination '*ṅe*'; for, otherwise, the latter by destroying the final '*a*' of *rāma* destroys that combination. The solution of the difficulty thus involved is found when we see that Pāṇini himself has used such expression as *kaṣṭāya* (Pāṇ. Sū. III.i. 18).

17. vṛttikṛtā tu pūrvavipratiṣedhena inātoḥ kritayos sannipātaparibhāṣāyā anityatvam āśritya jarasi kṛte nirjarasina nirjarasād iti rūpe na tu nirjarasā nirjarasa iti kecid ity uktam. tathā hi bhisi nirjarasair iti rūpāntaram uktam. tadanusāribhiś ca ṣaṣṭhyekavacane nirjarasye'ty eva rūpaṁ svīkṛtam. etac ca bhāṣyaviruddham. S. Kau. pp. 51.2. Also the T.Bod thereunder.

18. Patañjali resorted to the principle of *yoga-vibhāga* which consists in splitting up the rules of Pāṇini into two parts, the first part being prescriptive and the second merely illustrative. For instance, dvitīyā-śritātītapatitagatātyastaprāptāpannaiḥ (Pāṇ. Sū II. i. 24) is divided into *dvitīyā*, meaning any word ending in *dvitīyā* (accusative) may be compounded with another word provided both of them are fit (*samartha*) for being compounded, and 'śritātītapatitagatātyastaprāptāpannaiḥ' meaning that words in the accusative are compounded with such words as *śrita*, *atīta*, etc. We can, thus, explain such forms as *arthalipsu* and others. But, for this *yoga-vibhāga*, it would have been difficult to offer justification for quite a large number of expressions occurring in the writings of eminent writers. It is for this reason that later grammarians have not laid down a large number of hard and fast rules for compounds. And, Bopadeva, the author of the *Mugdhabodha*, goes so far as to say that in the matter of *kṛt*, *taddhita* and *samāsa*, we must depend upon the use (kṛttaddhitasamāsānām abhidhānaṁ niyāmakam). The avowed object of Kātyāyana was to criticise Pāṇini and supply the deficiencies (uktānuktaduruktārthavyaktikāri tu vārttikam); but, Patañjali defends Pāṇini by trying to show that the sūtra, if properly understood, will be found to make provision for most of the forms that are not apparently sanctioned by Pāṇini. We may be permitted to point out in this connection that it has been the usual practice with Indian scholars to evolve a thing from the existing materials instead of seeking to create a new thing for themselves. The

different systems of Indian philosophy claiming to interpret the *Brahmasūtras* of Bādarāyaṇa in their favour is an instance to the point.

19. Pāṇ. Sū. VI. i. 85, *antādivac ca*, enjoins that in the case of assimilation of letters the substitute may be regarded as the last member of the first word or the first member of the last word. It should not, however, be supposed that this alternative choice may lead to confusion in some cases. For the grammarian replies that in all cases of doubt, the explanation of the masters will guide us in the proper direction: vyākhyānato viśeṣapratipattir na hi sandehād alakṣaṇam. PSS. *Paribhāṣā* I.

20. hare've'tyādi dṛṣṭvā ca vākyasphoṭaṁ viniścinu. VBS. 66

21. vastutas tu padaiḥ padārthabodhavad vākyena vākyārthabodha iti padārthaśaktiḥ padeṣv iva vākyārthaśaktir vākye'bhyupeye 'ti padasphoṭa-vākyasphoṭau vyavasthitau. op. cit., pp. 427-8

22. ānupūrvīparyavasitā tv ākāṅkṣā. ŚŚP., p. 14

23. tādṛśasākāṅkṣaniṣṭhabodhahetutvasyai'vā'smanmate vākyaśaktitvenā 'kāṅkṣāśaktir iti paribhāṣābhede 'pi vākyasphoṭasiddhir nirābādhā. VBSD., pp. 428-9

24. The cognition of the import of a sentence has been called a qualified knowledge; for, it involves the cognition of a particular substantive determined by a particular attribute in a particular relation. Now, prior to the verbal knowledge, either the substantive or the attribute may be known but not both. Both are cognised only at the time of the verbal knowledge.

25. nanu vākyārthasyā 'pūrvatvāt kathaṁ tatra saṅketagrahaḥ. VBS., p. 432

26. The relation that subsists between a substantive and an attribute is known to be *apposition*. When two senses are thus related, they are expressed by two terms having the same case-ending : e.g., 'nīlo ghaṭaḥ'. Hence, Praśastapāda defines apposition as : ekavibhaktyantapadavācyatvaṁ sāmānādhikaraṇyam. The grammarian, however, says that when two words with different connotations reside in the same substratum, the relation between them is called *apposition*. Thus, the connotation of *nīla*, in the opinion of the grammarian, is 'blue colour' and that of *ghaṭa* is 'the class of jars' (*ghaṭatva-jāti*); and both of them can reside in the same substratum, viz., *ghaṭa*, the individual jar. So, the two words are said to be in apposition with each other. We may very well refer to the definition of apposition as set forth by Nāgeśabhaṭṭa under Pāṇ. Sū. I.ii. 42: bhinnapravṛttinimittaprayuktasyā 'nekasya śabdasyai' kasminn arthe vṛttis sāmānādhikaraṇyam. (MBP., Vol. II, p. 37).

27. Jagadīśa anticipates the objection but does not find out any new line of defence. He dogmatically maintains that the import of a term may at times be construed with a portion of the import of another term. (bahuvrīhāv apy abhedena padārthaikadeśānvayabodhasya vyutpattivaicitryeṇa sambhavāt. ŚŚP., p. 66)

28. sāmarthyañ ca dvividhaṁ vyapekṣālakṣaṇam ekārthībhāvalakṣaṇañ ce'ti. ekārthībhāvas tu rājapuruṣa ityādivṛttāv eva. T. Bod., p. 154

29. bahūnāṁ vṛttidharmāṇāṁ vacanair eva sādhane,
syān mahad gauravaṁ tasmād ekārthībhāva āśritaḥ.
cakārādiniṣedho'tha bahuvyutpattibhañjnam,
kartavyaṁ te nyāyasiddhaṁ tv asmākaṁ tad iti sthitam.

30. The Vedas have been divided into *mantras* and *brāhmaṇas*; and the latter again, into *vidhis* and *arthavādas*. Āpastamba says that *vidhi* refers to those passages which contain injunctions while the rest are known as *arthavāda*. ĀPB., 32-3

31. vidhinā tv ekavākyatvāt stutyarthena vidhīnāṁ syuḥ. MS. I. ii.7
Also : vidhyarthavādau sākāṅkṣau prāśastyapuruṣārthayoḥ,
tenai'kavākyatā tasmād vādānāṁ dharmamānatā. JNM. I ii. 1

32. śakyatva iva śaktatve jāter lāghavam iṣyatām,
aupādhiko vā bhedo'stu varṇānāṁ tāramandravat. VBS. 71
Also : śakyatāvacchedikāyā jāter vācyatvavat śaktatāvacchedikāyā jāter vācakatvam iti mate varṇapadavākyabhedena trividho jātisphoṭaḥ. SC., p. 1

33. pade varṇā na vidyante varṇeṣv avayavā iva,
vākyāt padānām atyantaṁ praviveko na kaścana. VP. I. 73

34. upāyāś śikṣmāṇānāṁ bālānām upalālanāḥ,
asatye vartmani sthitvā tatas satyaṁ samīhate. V.P. II. 240
Also : śāstreṣu prakriyābhedair avidyai'vo'pavarṇyate, V.P. II. 235

35. kathaṁ punar avidyāvadviṣayāṇi pratyakṣādīni pramāṇāni śāstrāṇi ce'ti. Śār. Bh., pp. 40-1
Also : dve satye samupāśritya buddhānāṁ dharmadeśanā,
lokasaṁvṛtisatyañ ca satyañ ca paramārthataḥ. MK. XXIV. 8

36. kecid āhur anavayavam eva vākyam anādyavidyopadarśitālīkavarṇapadavibhāgamasya nimittam. TB., p. 1

37. tad evā' smābhis sakhaṇḍapadasphoṭatvena vyavahriyate. khaṇḍaśaktyanusandhānapūrvakakośādinā samudāyaśaktigrahāt. yasya tu vyākaraṇajñānaśūnyasya kevalavyavahāreṇa samudāyaśaktigrahas tasya sa evā 'khaṇḍasphoṭaḥ. SC., p. 6

CHAPTER FOUR

1. pratyakṣānumānāgamāḥ pramāṇāni. YS. 1. 7
2. sábdāt tadarthaviṣayā vṛttiś śrotur āgamaḥ. YSV thereunder.
3. taddarśanakāruṇyakaraṇapāṭavābhisambandha āptis tayā saha vartata ity āptaḥ. Vācaspati thereunder.
4. āptena dṛṣṭo 'numito vā'rthaḥ paratra svabodhasaṅkrāntaye śabdeno' padiśyate. YSV. under YS I. 7
5. āptacittavartijñānasadṛśasya jñānasya śrotṛcitte samutpādaḥ. Vācaspati thereunder.
6. tathai'vā'yaṁ śrutismṛtilakṣaṇas sarvaiś śiṣṭaiḥ parigṛhīta āgamaḥ. com. under VPS.I. 41;
7. VP. I. 5
8. yeṣāṁ tv ayaṁ śākhāpravibhāgo vicchedena punaḥ punar bhavatī'ty āgamaḥ, com. under VPS. I. 6
yeṣām tu darśanaṁ brahmaṇaḥ prathamato veda ekarūpa eva vivartate, so dhyetṝnām aśakteḥ pravibhaktas sa punar upasaṁhṛtabhedo bhavatī 'ti punaś ca bhidyata iti. com. under VP.I.6 (p. 27)
9. sādhutvajñānaviṣayā sai'ṣā vyākaraṇasmṛtiḥ,
avicchedena śiṣṭānām idam smṛtinibandhanam. VP. I. 143
tasmān nibadhyate śiṣṭais sādhutvaviṣayā smṛtiḥ. op. cit. I. 29
antarhitām api ca tatsaṁskṛtāntaḥkaraṇās santaḥ punaḥ punas smṛtvā upanibadhnanti. com. under VPS I. 29 (p. 84)

10. bhraṣṭo vyākaraṇāgamaḥ. VP. II. 488; parvatād āgamaṁ labdhvā. op. cit., II. 489; āgamasaṁgrahaḥ op cit. II. 490. bhinnair āgama-darśanaiḥ op. cit., II 492; purāṇair āgamair vinā op. cit. II. 493
11. śiṣṭāṇām yad idam avicchinnapāramparyam smaraṇam sa āgamaḥ, com. under VPS I. 27'.
12. śiṣṭebhya āgamāt siddhās sādhavo dharmasādhanam,
arthapratyāyanābhede viparītās tv asādhavaḥ. VP. I. 27
13. idam puṇyam idaṁ pāpam ity etasmin padadvaye
ācaṇḍālaṁ manuṣyāṇāṁ samaṁ śāstraprayojanam. VP. I. 40
dharmaṁ praty anyasyo 'pāyabhāvaṁ nirākaroti. com. under VP. I. 30
na cā'gamād ṛte dharmas tarkeṇa vyavatiṣṭhate. VP. I.30
14. ṛṣīṇām api yaj jñānaṃ tad apy āgamapūrvakam. loc. cit.
15. *Uttararāmacarita* IV. 18
16. Dr. S. Mookerjee is probably obsessed with the idea that the water of a well may have a tepid temperature only and cannot be very hot. He seems to have forgotten that there are springs which are *atyuṣṇa* (cp. valāhakāgnikuṇḍādiṣu tadrūpāṇām evā 'tyuṣṇa upalabhyate; also, udakasthānam agnikuṇḍaṁ rājagṛhādiṣu (Rājgir is in the province of Bihar). VPS. P. 89
17. Dr. Iyer's translation is misleading; he seems to forget that *abhra* (com. under VPS. I. 33) means mica and not cloud as he suggests.
18. See VP I. 30-42
19. āvirbhūtaprakāśānām anupaplutacetasām,
atītānāgatajñānaṁ pratyakṣān na viśiṣyate. VP. I. 30
20. *The Buddhist Philosophy of Universal Flux*. Ch. XXIV
21. iti nyāyo bahuvidhas tarkeṇa pravibhajyate. VP. I. 136
22. vedaśāstrāvirodhī ca tarkaś cakṣur apaśyatām.
rūpamātrād dhi vākyārthaḥ kevalān nā 'vatiṣṭhate. VP. I. 135
23. śābdānām eva sā śaktis tarko yaḥ puruṣāśrayah. VP. I. 139
Also, com. thereunder.
24. uta tvaḥ paśyan na dadarśa vācam,
uta tvaḥ śṛṇvan na śṛṇoty enām,
uto tv asmai tanvaṁ visasre,
jāye'va patye uśatī suvāsāḥ.

yathā khalu ṛtusnātā jāyā prāktanaṁ rajodūṣitaṁ vasanam apāsya suvāsās satī sambhogecchuḥ praṇayaprakarṣāpanīyamānatrapā tasminn api vāsasi śanais sraṁsamāne svāṁ tanum anavayavena pariṇāyakāya vivṛṇute, tadvad iyaṁ vāṇī vyākaraṇatīrthasnānāpanītaduṣṭaśabdācchādanā prayoga-niyamānugamyamānaśobhanavarṇavasanā satī uśatī prasīdantī yogābhyā-sarūpapraṇayātiśayaśithilīkṛtājñānalajjā varṇākāraviparyāsavasane' pi śanais sraṁsamāṇe svāṁ tanum anavayavena śābdikapariṇāyakāya vivṛṇute. SS(Bh,) pp. 28-9.

25. Cp. SSN. 211-42.
26. vyadarśi yuktyāgamasaṁśrayeṇa. SS., 36.
Also : tathā 'uta tvaḥ paśyan' ityādimantravarṇānusāreṇa varṇātiriktaṁ padatattvam adhyavasīyata iti varṇayanti. Gop., p. 262.
27. Sāṅ. Sū., V. 57, and *vṛtti* thereunder.
28. *Philosophy of Sanskrit Grammar*, pp. 110-1
29. op. cit, p. 125.
30. VPS. I. 20
31. VP. I. 144 and com. thereunder.

REFERENCES

PRIMARY SOURCES

1. Nyāya-mañjarī : Jayantabhaṭṭa.
2. Ślokavārttika (Sphoṭa-vāda, śabdanityatādhikaraṇa) : Kumārila-bhaṭṭa.
3. Sphoṭa-candrikā : Mauni Śrī Kṛṣṇabhaṭṭa. Ed. M. S. Bakre, Bombay, 1913.
4. Sphoṭa-candrikā : Com. on Śabdakaustubha of Bhaṭṭojidīkṣita, Jayakṛṣṇamauni: Ed. V. P. Dvivedin and G. S. Mokate Vol. 2 Chowkhamba Sanskrit series 2. 1898-1917.
5. Sphoṭa-niraṇaya : Kauṇḍabhaṭṭa. Ed. S. D. Joshi, Poona. 1967.
6. Sphoṭa-siddhi : Maṇḍana-miśra with Gopālikā of Ṛṣiputraparameśvara. Ed. S. K. Ramanatha Sastri. Madras, 1931.
7. Sphoṭa-siddhi : Bharata-miśra. Ed. Sambasiva Sastri, K. Trivandrum. 1927.
8. Sphoṭa-siddhi-nyāyavicāra : Unknown author. Ed. Ganapathi Sastri. Trivandrum 1917.
9. Sphoṭa-tattva-nirūpaṇa : Śeṣakṛṣṇa. Bombay. 1913.
10. Sphoṭa-vāda: Nāgeśabhaṭṭa. Ed. V. Krishnamacarya. Madras. 1946.
11. Tattva-bindu : Introduction by Sastri V. A. R. Annamalai University. 1936.
12. Vaiyākaraṇa-siddhānta-laghumañjūṣā : Nāgeśabhaṭṭa. Benares. 1946.

SECONDARY SOURCES

1. Bruno Liebich : "Über den Sphoṭa" *ZDMG*, 1923, pp. 208 ff.
2. Bhattacharya, B. : "Constitution of words : Sphoṭa theory and its Opponents" *Our Heritage*. 4. 1956. pp. 217-226.
3. Chakravarti, P. C. : Philosophy of Sanskrit Grammar, Calcutta University, Calcutta.
4. Dayananda, Swamin : "Varṇa-sphoṭa-nirūpaṇa" *Festschrift Satkari Mookerji*, pp. 590-93.
5. Iyer, K. A. S. : "Bhartṛhari-abhipretaḥ Śabdārtha-sambandhaḥ" *Viśva-saṁskṛtam* (Hoshiarpur) 4. pp. 207-19.
   " " : "The doctrine of Sphoṭa" J. of the *Ganganath Jha* Research Institute. Vol. 5 pp. 121-147.
   " " : *Sphoṭa siddhi* (tr.) Poona 1966.
6. Jha Maninath : "Sphoṭavāda in Sanskrit" PAIOC 14.4 sum 1948. pp. 32-33.
7. Pandeya, Kalicaran : "The theory of Śabda-Brahman and Sphoṭa" *J. of the Ganganatha Jha Institute* Vol. 17. 1961. pp. 253-256.
8. Raja K. K. "Sphoṭa, the theory of Linguistic symbols" Adyar library Bulletin Vol. 20. 1956. pp. 84-118.
9. Sarma Raghunatha : *Citranibandhāvaliḥ*, Motilal Banarsidass, 1964.
10. Sastri Kapiladeva "Vaiyākaraṇānāṁ Sphoṭavādaḥ" *Viśvasaṁskritam* 4. 1968, pp. 40-51.
11. Sastri V. A. R. "The Doctrine of Sphoṭa" Journal of Annamalai University, Vol. 1.

... ...

Note

The above list has been prepared on the advice of the author's young friend, Dr. Kunjunni Raja, Professor of Sanskrit, Madras University.